THE ESSENTIAL
MIXER COOKBOOK

THE ESSENTIAL
MIXER COOKBOOK

150 EFFORTLESS RECIPES FOR YOUR STAND MIXER
AND ALL OF ITS ATTACHMENTS

whitecap

KAY HALSEY

KEY TO KITCHENAID ATTACHMENTS

 wire whip

 flat beater

 dough hook

 food grinder

 strainer

 pasta maker

 sausage stuffer

 citrus juicer

 grain mill

ROTOR SLICER/SHREDDER

 medium shredding cone

 coarse shredding cone

 slicing cone

 fine shredding cone

 stripping cone

 potato grating cone

BLENDER SPEED SETTINGS

 blender

 stir

 chop

 mix

 purée

 liquefy

MEASURES AND ABBREVIATIONS

The following abbreviations have been used in the recipes:

Tbsp = tablespoon
tsp = teaspoon
oz = ounces
lb = pound

NOTE

All spoon measurements used throughout this book are level unless otherwise specified.

WARNING

Because of the slight risk of salmonella, raw or lightly cooked eggs should not be served to the very young, the ill or elderly, or to pregnant women.

A QUINTET BOOK

Copyright © 2003 Quintet Publishing Ltd

This book was designed and produced by
Quintet Publishing Limited
6 Blundell Street
London N7 9BH

This edition published in the U.S. and Canada by Whitecap Books Ltd. For more information, contact Whitecap Books, 351 Lynn Avenue, North Vancouver, British Columbia, Canada, V7J 2C4.

ISBN 1-55285-503-1

Publisher: Oliver Salzmann
Managing Editor: Diana Steedman
Text editors: Margaret Gilbey, Kay Halsey
Creative Director: Richard Dewing
Design: Janis Utton, Sharanjit Dhol, Tristan de Lancey
Photography: Tim Ferguson Hill, Ian Garlick
Food Styling: Jacqueline Bellefontaine, Christine Rodrigues

Color separation by Chroma Graphics Pte Ltd, Singapore
Printed in Singapore by Star Standard Industries (Pte) Ltd.

ACKNOWLEDGMENTS

The Publishers are grateful to the following for assistance, guidance, and support provided in the production of this book, especially to Gina Steer, Catherine Atkinson, Elizabeth Ramjoué, Fiona Ford, Mauro Spagnol, Catherine Masciocchi, Katie Bishop, Rosemary Moon, Jenny Stacey, for their work with the recipes; and to Paul Judge for use of his kitchen for photography.

CONTENTS

KITCHENAID®—A LEGEND in professional kitchens and restaurants, the KitchenAid® mixer was developed in

1919 and has stood the test of time to become an American icon. A design classic, its beauty lies in its power and workmanlike efficiency. All-metal, robust, and stable, the machine beats, whisks, stirs, kneads, and mixes – performing the most repetitive, time-consuming, and heavy jobs in the kitchen with a graceful ease.

In 1908, the same year that Henry Ford first produced his Model T, Herbert Johnston, an engineer from Ohio, found himself watching a baker laboriously mixing his bread dough with a heavy iron spoon. The new century had imbued the country with a spirit of enterprise and discovery, and Herbert felt sure he could find a way of mechanizing this heavy work. He began to work on developing what would soon become the world's first commercial mixer.

His first attempt to create a mixer, the Hobart model H, went on the market in 1914 and was a giant, with a huge 16-gallon capacity. Its commercial potential was soon realized and eager customers ranged from chains of bakeries to the US Navy, which by 1917 had made it standard equipment on the galleys of all its ships. The success of the H model inspired Hobart's engineers to start thinking about creating a mixer for home use.

During World War I Hobart, along with most other American manufacturers, converted their production lines to war work. So it was not until after the War, on the brink of the peace and prosperity of the Roaring Twenties, that thought turned again to producing a mixer for the home. In 1919, that dream became a reality and the Hobart model H-5, the first domestic mixer, broke on to the market. Named the "KitchenAid," the model was a direct descendant of Hobart's professional models and a real breakthrough. Of extremely high quality, the KitchenAid® mixers were made with real attention to detail, and only four machines a day rolled off the company's assembly line in Springfield, Ohio. However, the KitchenAid mixer was by no means cheap – priced at $189.50 it cost the equivalent of $1,500 in today's dollars.

Throughout the 1920s, the company continued to make new models, refining the design to deliver the same quality at a lower price. In 1927 they launched their G model, which was to mark the beginning of a new era of significant growth for the company, selling 20,000 models in just three years. Ever glamorous, the new KitchenAid mixer wowed America, and its famous users ranged from Henry Ford to Ginger Rogers and Marion Davies.

Even with the G model doing so well, the Depression in the 1930s forced KitchenAid to keep searching for ways to produce ever better-value models. In a masterful move in 1936, the world-acclaimed designer Egmont Arens was commissioned to create three new models for the company. His K models were to become design icons, winning many awards and earning a place in

design museums throughout the world. In 1955, KitchenAid caused a sensation at the Atlantic City Housewares Show when the K model first appeared in a range of colors – Petal Pink, Sunny Yellow, Island Green, Satin Chrome, and Antique Copper. It was certainly a far cry from the workmanlike colors of the original machines.

Up to this day, the basic design remains virtually unchanged and the attachments that came with Egmont Arens' 1936 machine could in fact be used in a machine bought today. The current palette of exciting colors was introduced as recently as 1994, and the KitchenAid mixer can now be bought in Imperial Red, Cobalt Blue, Onyx Black, Almond Cream, Majestic Yellow, Matt Gray, Brushed Nickel, Chrome, and White.

So what has made the KitchenAid mixer such a classic design and the world's top household mixer?

Just looking at the machine, the first reason is obvious. The KitchenAid mixer is made of solid metal with a tough enamel finish that is made to last. As well as looking good, this means the machine is stable, tough, and robust. Initially developed for the workload of busy professional kitchens, KitchenAid mixers are made to be used hard.

Turn on your machine and you'll see the KitchenAid mixer's unique planetary mixing method kick into action. Patented as part of the original 1919 design, the machine looks effortlessly graceful as the flat beater, wire whip, or dough hook turns around the mixer bowl, while the planetary turns the opposite way, blending ingredients thoroughly and reaching right into every part of the bowl.

And the force that is making your KitchenAid mixer work so efficiently is its impressive 300 Watts of power, which allows the 10-speed, gear-driven motor to steadily ease you through from gentle stirring to high-speed whipping. The result is a quiet, reliable, and efficient machine.

After your cake is in the oven, the KitchenAid mixer's timeless design and smooth, rounded edges make it easy to clean, with no lids or blades to trap food.

But your KitchenAid mixer doesn't stop there. Additional attachments, which fit easily in and out of a single hub, allow the machine to do all the jobs of a food processor and more. Chopping, shredding, or slicing, you can grind your own meat or your own flour, and if you want, your KitchenAid mixer can transform itself into a pasta or sausage maker, a strainer, or even your own juicer.

GETTING TO KNOW YOUR KITCHENAID® MIXER Every time you use

your KitchenAid mixer you'll get to know it a little better and learn what it does best. Don't only use recipes written for the KitchenAid mixer – it will speed up almost any food preparation. You can convert all your favorite recipes using just your own observations and experience.

The Speed Control Guide in your manual will help you, and the recipes written especially for the KitchenAid mixer in this book are a good place to start getting a feeling for correct timings and consistencies.

PROFESSIONAL TIPS When mixing, start on the slowest speed and gradually increase to the required speed to prevent too much splashing, especially when there is a large amount of liquid ingredients. Use the Speed Control Guide to help you decide which speed is suitable for each job and attachment. If you are unsure, use a slower speed and work up gradually. Use the Pouring Shield to make adding ingredients while the machine is operating less messy. The KitchenAid mixer is powerful, and you will find that you probably need to adjust down the mixing times in all your recipes to avoid overbeating.

When whisking, start on the slowest speed and gradually increase the speed until the mixture is frothy. You can then increase it further to a fast whisking speed. However, do not whisk too quickly as this will in fact incorporate less air, leading to a dense and heavy mixture. If whisking eggs, make sure they are at room temperature. If whipping cream, chill the mixer bowl first and keep the cream in the refrigerator until ready to mix. Be careful not to overwhip, as cream can thicken very quickly, and don't use the wire whip for recipes with butter or margarine in them as this can get stuck in the wire whip.

When making bread, you can start by mixing the ingredients together using the flat beater, especially if you're only making a small quantity of dough, as it is more efficient for straightforward mixing than the dough hook. Change to the dough hook to mix in the liquid, adding it gradually so it doesn't form a pool that might slow down the mixing. When the dough starts to form a ball, knead for a few minutes until smooth and elastic. You can just leave the bread to prove in the bowl, covered with the plastic lid, which will pop off when the bread rises.

When adding extra ingredients, add as close to the side of the bowl as possible, not directly into the moving beater (the pouring shield will help you do this). When adding solid ingredients such as nuts, raisins, or candied fruits into a batter, always fold them in during the last few seconds of mixing on the slowest speed to prevent the air being knocked out.

When you are not using your machine, leave it on the counter top, storing the attachments in the bowl with the plastic cover on to keep it all dust-free and ready-to-use.

THE FLAT BEATER The workhorse of your KitchenAid mixer, the flat beater is the attachment to turn to for all kinds of mixing. Able to deal with any normal to heavy mixtures, it is of course great for making cakes, cookies, and pastry, deftly cutting in soft butter or margarine or blending a mixture. However, the flat beater can mash vegetables or whip up dips and pâtés; evenly blend together meatloaf and meatballs; or stir together a shiny butter cream. Try it for any mixture that needs to be quickly stirred together or thoroughly blended.

THE WIRE WHIP is the attachment to use when you need to incorporate some air into your mixture. It can whip cream; whisk eggs to create meringues, ice creams, mousses, and mayonnaise; and is also great for applying a little first-aid to lumpy sauces and custards. Use the wire whip rather than the flat beater when you want to make whisked sponges – light cakes made without fat – and fluffy egg white icings.

THE DOUGH HOOK is for making and kneading doughs. If you want to wake up to the smell of home-made bread, the dough hook can mix and knead any kind, from focaccia to rye; dinner rolls to thin-crust pizzas.. The dough hook is also used to make pasta dough. And if you enjoy baking your own cakes, a great tip is to use the dough hook rather than the beater to stir the fruit and nuts into the cake mix.

ABOVE LEFT: *Rotor Slicer/Shredder* **ABOVE MIDDLE:** *Food grinder with food tray, strainer, and sausage maker accessories* **ABOVE RIGHT:** *Grain mill*

ATTACHMENTS AND ACCESSORIES

ROTOR SLICER/SHREDDER This attachment is so useful it is probably used more frequently than any other in the recipes. Store it with the sharp slicing drum in place and it'll be ready to go when you need to slice a few onions for a sauce or some potatoes for a topping. The Rotor Slicer/Shredder comes with three drums: a medium and a coarse shredding drum, and a slicing drum. All three are great for making salads, especially coleslaw; slicing potatoes for gratins; shredding fruit for pies; shredding cheese; and slicing big quantities of raw or cooked vegetables for cooking. If you need to switch from slicing to shredding in the middle of a recipe, you don't have to remove the attachment from your KitchenAid mixer, just change the cone, and you can even shred straight into the same bowl. The shredding cones can also do thin strips of vegetables — just turn your vegetable around and put it into the machine horizontally.

OPTIONAL CONES There are three additional cones for use with the Rotor Slicer/Shredder for more precision slicing and shredding. The fine shredding cone makes light work of cheese, chocolate, nuts, and bread, there is a potato grating cone and a stripping cone for julienne-style vegetables.

FOOD GRINDER The food grinder is much more than just a great grinder. This attachment is the equivalent of the main blade in a food processor and it can chop and roughly liquidize as well as grind. Use it, of course, for grinding meat and fish. It allows you to choose exactly the cut and quality you want and has a choice of a coarse or fine grinding plate for making your own charcuterie, from sausages to pâtés, or some high-quality home-made burgers for your barbecue. But use it also to make bread crumbs or cheesecake bases; shred firm fruit and cheese; shred a carrot very fine or grind an onion to disappear into a sauce. If you want to make a soup or sauce with a rough, country-style texture, use this attachment rather than the strainer. The food grinder is also the body for the strainer and the sausage maker.

FOOD TRAY If you process large volumes of fruits, vegetables, or meats, the food tray is one accessory you'll definitely want to own. It easily attaches on to the food grinder to provide a much larger capacity to both the grinder and the strainer, allowing you to fill the food tray up with more fruit or vegetables for processing without having to refill so often.

SAUSAGE STUFFER The sausage stuffer attaches to the food grinder and the two work together to produce delicious old-fashioned, home-made sausages and sausage meat that can be made from quality cuts of meat. The sausage stuffer can produce any sausages, not just the classic meat varieties, but vegetarian or uncased ones too. Once made, sausages are quick to cook and make an easy, simple supper.

ABOVE LEFT: *Pasta maker* **ABOVE MIDDLE:** *Citrus juicer* **ABOVE RIGHT:** *Can opener*

FRUIT/VEGETABLE STRAINER While the food grinder can produce a rough purée, it is the strainer that will break fruit and vegetables down to the smoothest pulp. Attaching to the food grinder, the strainer can purée any soft fruits and cooked vegetables, while separating out pips, stems, and skins. It will make a silky smooth soup or sauce, or if you want a bit more texture, you can just mix the smooth and rough pulps back together again. Perfect for preparing large quantities of fruit for a sorbet, coulis, or a smooth jelly jam, the strainer allows you to make the most of a summer glut of fresh fruit. It also provides a wonderfully easy way of preparing your own healthy baby food.

CITRUS JUICER Perfect for preparing large quantities of orange, grapefruit, lemon, or lime juice in no time at all for everything from sorbets to marmalade to icy homemade lemonade. So easy to use, you can increase your daily fruit intake by creating a healthy juice to drink every day. Kick-start your morning with freshly squeezed orange, or add citrus juice to your favorite breakfast smoothie to make a sensational and healthy sunrise drink.

POURING SHIELD The pouring shield makes adding ingredients while mixing easy. Sitting on the rim of the mixer bowl, the pouring spout directs the food to the sides when adding new ingredients and the shield prevents any splashing. Transparent, it also gives you a full view of the ingredients in the bowl.

PASTA MAKER This beautifully made, traditional-style pasta machine makes daily homemade pasta a reality. Crafted out of chromed metal in Italy by Marcato, who also produce hand-operated machines, it is easy and fun to use. The roller and two cutters allow you to make any kind of flat pasta, from sheets of lasagne to strips of tagliatelle and even threads of angel hair pasta. And it's quick – the flat beater whips up the pasta dough, the dough hook kneads it, then the pasta rollers do all the work while you use both hands to thread the sheets through until they are as smooth, thin, and wide as required. The cutters can then cut the sheets into lengths of spaghetti or noodles to be cooked right away.

GRAIN MILL The grain mill transforms your KitchenAid mixer into a new machine – a mill that can grind grains from wheat and rye to rice and corn to produce the freshest flour for baking delicious and nutritious whole grain breads, muffins, and cakes. It can also create more unusual flours from grains, beans, or legumes, such as besan flour from garbanzo beans. Adjust it to mill anything from a fine flour to coarsely cracked grains.

CAN OPENER Made from solid metal, this heavy-duty attachment holds your can securely in place to open, while a magnet picks up the lid after opening. It can tackle all sizes of tins and if you keep your mixer out on the counter – you can have this as your default attachment.

THE KITCHENAID® BLENDER
With its "pulse at any speed" feature, the blender is a worthwhile additional appliance to complement the KitchenAid stand mixer.

THE BLENDER uses power and speed to blend, shake, crush, mix, and chop its way through smoothies and milkshakes, soups, bread crumbs, herbs, and wonderful crushed ice cocktails. It can produce baby food to just the consistency your child likes it, as well as being a quick way of making up a weekend breakfast pancake batter, a fresh herb salad dressing, an icy sorbet, or a quick sauce for a weeknight pasta. It's so powerful that few jobs take more than 30 seconds, and it can transform a handful of nuts into homemade peanut butter in under a minute.

The KitchenAid blender is a solid, powerful machine – with a stable all-metal base and heavy-duty glass jar. The unique asymmetric and blunt blade powers, rather than splices, its way through ingredients, throwing the food up and around the jar so that it blends together thoroughly, without the mixture catching underneath the blade. The 10-speed touch-button control pad has easy-to-use symbols that take you through from stirring and ice-crushing to liquifying, and the mixing sensor will automatically adjust your speed when it senses more power is needed.

The ultimate ice-crusher, your KitchenAid blender can make fantastic icy fruit drinks and frozen cocktails – crushing hard ice to snow and melting cubes to slush in seconds. Made for professional barmen, the cap for the jar is also a quick measuring jug for small amounts of lime juice and sugar syrup.

PROFESSIONAL TIPS When blending, always start on the slowest speed to prevent splashing and mix everything together thoroughly, then just press the next button when you want to move up to a higher speed.

When making bread crumbs, process the pieces of bread about five times, for a few seconds each time, at a chop speed ⊙.

When chopping fruits and vegetables, cut into chunks and process a few times on a stir or chop speed ⊙⊙ with the pulse button, checking the consistency so as not to overprocess. If you want to take it further to a purée, you'll need to add a little liquid and process at a purée speed ⊙.

When adding extra ingredients while the KitchenAid blender is operating, remove the ingredient cap and add through the top. Keep the machine on one of the two lowest speeds (stir and chop ⊙⊙) and stop if the ingredients are hot or the jar is full. When making mayonnaise, it can help to create a small waxed paper cone for the oil to pour slowly down.

RECIPE INDEX

Recipe	1	2	3	4	5	6	7	8	9	10	11	Country
TZATZIKI p.14	•			•								GREECE
HUMMUS p.14		•				•						LEBANON
GUACAMOLE p.15	•											MEXICO
TARAMASALATA p.15										•		GREECE
TEMPURA p.17	•	•										JAPAN
TOMATO AND ANCHOVY BRUSCHETTA p.18	•			•								ITALY
BLINIS p.18	•	•	•									RUSSIA
TAPENADE CROSTINI p.19	•				•							ITALY
COUNTRY PORK PÂTÉ p.21	•			•	•							INTERNATIONAL
MAYONNAISE p.22		•										FRANCE
AÏOLI p.22		•										FRANCE
CELERIAC REMOULADE p.23		•		•								FRANCE
WHITE CABBAGE AND APPLE SALAD p.24	•			•								GERMANY
RED CABBAGE SALAD p.25	•			•								GERMANY
ICED ZUCCHINI SOUP WITH SAGE p.26				•						•		FRANCE
PEA SOUP p.28				•	•							THE NETHERLANDS
POTATO SOUP p.29				•	•							GERMANY
ONION SOUP GRATINÉE p.29				•								FRANCE
GAZPACHO p.30	•			•								SPAIN
MINESTRONE WITH PESTO p.31				•								ITALY
RED PEPPER AND CHILI SOUP p.32										•		MEXICO
PIZZA MARGHERITA p.35	•		•	•								ITALY
BÉCHAMEL SAUCE p.36				•								FRANCE
PESTO p.36				•						•		ITALY
TOMATO PASSATA p.37				•		•						ITALY
BOLOGNESE SAUCE p.37				•	•							ITALY
BASIC PASTA DOUGH p.38	•		•				•					ITALY
LINGUINE WITH GARLIC AND OIL p.40							•					ITALY
TAGLIATELLE WITH PARMESAN AND CILANTRO SAUCE p.41	•		•				•			•		INTERNATIONAL
EGGPLANT AND PARMESAN LASAGNE p.42				•			•					ITALY
PEPPERS AND BROCCOLI LASAGNE p.43				•			•					INTERNATIONAL
CRAB AND GREEN ONION CANNELLONI p.44				•			•					INTERNATIONAL
SPINACH, MUSHROOM, AND RICOTTA CANNELLONI p.45	•			•			•					ITALY
RAVIOLI p.46				•	•		•					ITALY
BEEF AND PORK POCKETS p.47	•				•		•					GERMANY
TORTELLINI WITH SMOKED SALMON AND DILL WEED p.48	•			•			•					INTERNATIONAL
SPINACH AND PARMESAN GNOCCHI p.50	•			•								ITALY
FETTUCCINE ALLA ROMANA p.51				•			•					ITALY
SPÄTZLE p.52	•			•								GERMANY
CRAB CAKES WITH MANGO SAMBAL p.55	•	•		•								MALAYSIA
TERRINE OF FISH p.56	•											SPAIN
FISH BALLS p.57	•				•							NORWAY
LAKSA p.58				•								MALAYSIA
SHRIMP AND GREEN ONION CRÊPES p.59	•			•								THAILAND
POACHED SALMON p.60				•								GREAT BRITAIN
CHICKEN, BELL PEPPER, AND MUSHROOM PARCELS p.62	•			•								GREAT BRITAIN
TURKEY WITH GARBANZO PATTIES p.63	•			•								MOROCCO
CHICKEN TANDOORI p.64				•								INDIA
CHICKEN WITH BELL PEPPERS p.65				•								THAILAND
LAMB EN CROÛTE p.66	•											FRANCE
PORK WITH CALVADOS AND APPLES p.68				•								FRANCE
VEAL IN TOMATO SAUCE p.69		•		•	•							ITALY
MEAT CAKES p.70	•			•								NORWAY
FILET AMÈRICAIN WITH BELGIAN FRITES p.72	•											BELGIUM
QUICHE LORRAINE p.73	•			•								FRANCE
MEATBALLS p.74	•			•	•							ITALY
SWEDISH MEATBALLS p.75	•			•	•							SWEDEN
SPICY SAUSAGES p.76	•				•			•				GERMANY
BRATWURST p.76	•				•			•				GERMANY
BABY CHICKEN WITH CARROTS p.78										•		BABY FOOD
BABY PEACH FOOL p.78										•		BABY FOOD
MASHED POTATOES p.80	•											IRELAND
COLCANNON p.80	•			•								IRELAND
HERB SAUCE WITH NEW POTATOES p.81	•			•								GERMANY
PISSALADIÈRE p.82			•	•								FRANCE
TORTA PASQUALINA p.84	•		•		•							ITALY
LITTLE STUFFED VEGETABLES p.86	•			•								FRANCE
VICHY CARROTS p.87				•								FRANCE
BRAISED RED CABBAGE p.88				•								GERMANY
BRAISED CELERY HEARTS p.88				•								FRANCE
NAPKIN DUMPLINGS p.89		•		•								GERMANY
GRATIN DAUPHINOIS p.90				•								FRANCE

Recipe	1	2	3	4	5	6	7	8	9	10	11	Country
ROSTI WITH APPLE SAUCE p.91				•								GERMANY
SWEET CUCUMBER PICKLE p.92				•								USA
PEACH CHUTNEY p.93				•	•							INDIA
ZUCCHINI AND TOMATO SAUTE p.94				•								INTERNATIONAL
ZUCCHINI WITH GARLIC p.94				•								INTERNATIONAL
LEEK AND ZUCCHINI QUICHE p.95	•			•								FRANCE
SPINACH AND CHEESE SOUFFLE p.96	•	•		•								FRANCE
GRANARY AND WALNUT BREAD p.99	•		•									GREAT BRITAIN
PAIN DE CAMPAGNE p.100			•									FRANCE
TOMATO AND OLIVE OIL BREAD p.101			•									ITALY
PITA BREAD p.101			•									ISRAEL
SOURDOUGH p.102	•		•									USA
CHALLAH p.105			•									ISRAEL
SODA BREAD p.105	•		•									IRELAND
RYE AND WHEAT BREAD p.106			•									GERMANY
FOCACCIA p.109			•									ITALY
PRETZELS p.110			•									GERMANY
CHAPATI p.111			•									INDIA
STOLLEN p.112	•		•									GERMANY
PANETTONE p.113			•									ITALY
SWEET BRAIDED ROLLS p.114			•									GERMANY
LEMON BRIOCHE p.115			•									FRANCE
CROISSANTS p.116	•		•	•								FRANCE
STRUDEL PASTRY p.118			•									GERMANY
FLAKY PASTRY p.118	•											FRANCE
CHOUX PASTRY p.119	•											FRANCE
PÂTE SABLÉE p.119	•											FRANCE
CRÈME PÂTISSIÈRE p.120		•										FRANCE
CRÈME MOUSSELINE p.120	•											FRANCE
CRÈME DESSERT p.121		•										FRANCE
CRÈME ANGLAISE p.121		•										FRANCE
CRÊPES p.122		•										FRANCE
BELGIAN WAFFLES p.123	•	•										BELGIUM
EMPEROR PANCAKES p.125	•	•										AUSTRIA
SWEET STEAMED DUMPLINGS p.126	•		•									GERMANY
FLOATING ISLANDS p.127		•										FRANCE
CHOCOLATE MOUSSE p.129		•										FRANCE
PLUM DUMPLINGS p.129			•									AUSTRIA
TARTE AU CITRON p.130	•								•			FRANCE
TARTE AU CHOCOLAT ET À LA FRAMBOISE p.132			•									FRANCE
POTS DE CRÈME AU CHOCOLAT p.133		•										FRANCE
RAISIN CHEESECAKE p.135	•											GERMANY
BLACK FOREST GATEAU p.136		•										GERMANY
DANISH CREAM PUDDING p.138		•										DENMARK
DANISH COOKIES p.138	•											DENMARK
ALMOND PASTRIES p.139	•											FRANCE
MERINGUES p.140		•										FRANCE
STRAWBERRY AND PASSION FRUIT PAVLOVA p.141		•										AUSTRALIA
APPLE STRUDEL p.143	•		•	•								GERMANY
TARTE TATIN p.144	•											FRANCE
APPLE PIE p.145	•			•								USA
LEMON AND LIME ICE CREAM p.145		•		•					•			ITALY
MANGO SORBET p.147	•					•						THAILAND
TIRAMISU p.148		•										ITALY
ZABAGLIONE p.148		•										ITALY
RASPBERRY PARFAIT p.149		•				•						FRANCE
FROZEN STRAWBERRY DAIQUIRI p.150											•	INTERNATIONAL
MARGARITA p.150											•	INTERNATIONAL
THE KITCHENAID BIRTHDAY CAKE p.153	•											INTERNATIONAL
GUGELHOPF p.154	•											FRANCE
GÂTEAU SAVOIE p.155		•										FRANCE
MARBLE CAKE p.156	•											GERMANY
ALMOND CAKES p.157		•		•	•							ITALY
APRICOT STREUSEL CAKE p.158	•	•	•									THE NETHERLANDS
PLUM CAKE p.159	•	•										GERMANY
SACHERTORTE p.160		•										AUSTRIA
ORANGE CHIFFON CAKE p.162	•	•							•			USA
WALNUT CAKE WITH SYRUP p.163	•	•			•							GREECE
APPLE FRITTERS p.164	•											SPAIN
COCONUT MACAROONS p.165		•										FRANCE
SHORTBREAD p.165	•											GREAT BRITAIN
LEBKUCHEN p.166	•			•								GERMANY
AUSTRIAN PASTRIES p.167	•		•	•								AUSTRIA
BLUEBERRY MUFFINS p.168	•											USA
GOLDEN RAISIN SCONES p.170	•											GREAT BRITAIN
DOUBLE CHOCOLATE BROWNIES p.171	•			•								USA
SPEKULATIUS p.172		•										AUSTRIA
BISCOTTI p.174	•	•	•									ITALY

APPETIZERS,
SALADS, AND SOUPS

TZATZIKI
Although the Greek dip tzatziki is usually served simply as a snack or an appetizer with bread, it is also a delicious accompaniment to broiled lamb chops or baked or broiled fish.

HUMMUS
A Middle-Eastern dish made from puréed garbanzo beans (chickpeas) and tahini, a sesame seed paste, and served as a dip with pita bread or with kabobs.

SERVES 6

Preparation time: 25 minutes plus
10 minutes chilling time

Attachments used

2 small cucumbers or 1 large firm cucumber, unpeeled

1 tsp salt

3 cups Greek yogurt

2–3 cloves garlic, minced

1 Tbsp white wine vinegar

2 Tbsp extra-virgin olive oil

Freshly ground black pepper

Few fresh mint leaves

1 With the coarse shredding cone on the Rotor Slicer/Shredder, on speed 4, shred the cucumber into a bowl, sprinkle with the salt, and leave for 10 minutes. Pour off any excess liquid, then place the cucumber into a strainer, and gently squeeze out any remaining water.

2 Transfer the cucumber to the mixer bowl and, using the flat beater, stir in the yogurt. Add the crushed garlic to the cucumber together with the vinegar and olive oil. Stir well, then add seasoning to taste, and chill in the refrigerator for 10 minutes. Serve chilled with the mint leaves on top.

SERVES 8

Preparation time: 10 minutes

Attachments used

2^1/$_2$ cups canned garbanzo beans (chickpeas), drained

^{1}/$_4$ cup cold water

^{1}/$_4$ cup fresh lemon juice

3 Tbsp tahini

3 cloves garlic, minced

^{1}/$_2$ tsp salt

^{1}/$_4$ tsp paprika (optional)

1 Using the fruit/vegetable strainer, on speed 4, strain the garbanzos into the mixer bowl. Return the waste to the strained garbanzos.

2 Add the water, lemon juice, tahini, garlic, salt, and paprika, if using. Using the wire whip, on speed 4, whisk for 1 minute. Stop and scrape the ingredients back down into the bowl. Increase to speed 10 and whisk for 1 minute, or until smooth. Serve with toasted pita bread.

GUACAMOLE An irresistible dip to enjoy with a

glass of something cool on a summer's evening, this famous fiery avocado

dip originates from Mexico.

TARAMASALATA This Greek meze dip is made

from tarama, salted coral-pink fish roe, originally taken from the gray mullet

but now more usually cod.

SERVES 4 TO 6

Preparation time: 15 minutes

Attachments used

2 large ripe avocados, cut in half and pitted

1 clove garlic

6 scallions, chopped fine

2 tomatoes, skinned, deseeded, and chopped

1 small green chile, chopped fine (optional)

1 Tbsp chopped fresh cilantro

Juice of 1 lime

Salt and freshly ground black pepper

SERVES 4 TO 6

Preparation time: 30 minutes plus

1 hour chilling time

Blender used

4–5 slices 2-day-old white bread, crusts discarded

4 Tbsp warm water

$1/2$ cup tarama

3 Tbsp olive oil

3–4 Tbsp lemon juice

Salt and freshly ground black pepper

1 Using a teaspoon, scrape the avocado flesh into the mixer bowl. Using the flat beater on speed 2, beat the avocado to a smooth purée.

2 Crush the garlic to a paste with a little salt and add to the mixer bowl with all the other ingredients. Beat again until well mixed. Chill until required.

1 Tear the bread into pieces, place in a bowl, and pour over the warm water. Leave for 10 minutes, then squeeze out any excess water and place into the blender. Blend briefly on mix speed. Add the tarama and blend, still on mix speed, until a paste is formed.

2 With the motor running, gradually add the olive oil and the lemon juice until a smooth purée is formed. Scrape into a bowl and add seasoning to taste, taking care not to add too much salt. Cover and chill in the refrigerator for 1 hour. When ready to serve, stir the taramasalata and spoon onto a plate. Serve with pita bread

TEMPURA
A Japanese dish where a light batter is used to coat pieces of seafood, meat, or vegetables, then deep-fried until it puffs up. It is served with a special dipping sauce made from soy and white wine vinegar.

SERVES 4

Preparation time: 1 hour

Cooking time: 30 minutes

Attachments used

8 oz large shrimp, peeled but tails left intact

6-oz piece middle-cut salmon fillet

1 red bell pepper, deseeded

1 yellow bell pepper, deseeded

1 large or 2 small zucchini

For the dipping sauce

2 Tbsp light soy sauce

1 Tbsp rice wine vinegar or white wine vinegar

1 Tbsp sweet chili sauce

Sliced fresh red chile, to garnish

For the batter

1 egg, separated

1^{1}/$_{2}$ cups ice-cold water

^{3}/$_{4}$ cup all-purpose flour

Salt

Sunflower oil, for deep-frying

1 Remove the thin black vein that runs down the back of each shrimp, rinse well, and dry on paper towels. Discard the skin and any bones from the salmon and cut into bite-size cubes, rinse and pat dry. Cut the peppers into thin strips, then cut the zucchini into strips. Blend all the dipping sauce ingredients together.

2 To make the batter, place the egg yolk in the mixer bowl and gradually pour the ice-cold water onto the egg yolk. Sift the flour then tip into the bowl with the salt. Using the flat beater, on speed 1, mix for 1 minute or until just incorporated. Pour into a large bowl.

3 Clean the mixer bowl and dry thoroughly, then using the wire whip, on speed 10, whisk the egg white until very soft peaks are formed. Gently fold the egg white into the batter.

In recipes where you need to fold whisked egg whites into a mixture that you have prepared with the flat beater, it is very useful to own a second mixer bowl so you can whip the egg whites without having to first transfer the mixture, and clean and dry the bowl.

4 Heat the oil to 375ºF in a wok or a deep-fat fryer and have ready a plate or tray lined with plenty of paper towels. Dip a few pieces of the seafood into the prepared batter, until lightly coated, allowing any excess to drip back into the bowl. Fry in the hot oil for 2 to 3 minutes or until thoroughly cooked. Remove from the oil and drain well on the paper towels.

5 When all the seafood is cooked, coat the vegetables in the remaining batter, and fry for 1 to 2 minutes. Drain well. Serve the tempura with the dipping sauce.

TOMATO AND ANCHOVY BRUSCHETTA Tuscan toasted bread, brushed with garlic and

topped with fresh tomatoes. For a more garlicky flavor, you could mince the garlic over the bread before spreading on the tomatoes.

SERVES 6

Preparation time: 8 minutes

Cooking time: 2 minutes

Attachments used

6 medium firm plum tomatoes, deseeded

2 anchovy fillets, drained

2 Tbsp extra-virgin olive oil

Salt and freshly ground black pepper

6 cloves garlic

6 thick slices baguette, or crusty bread, toasted

1 Use the Rotor Slicer/Shredder, fitted with the medium shredding cone, and shred the tomatoes and anchovies, on speed 4, into the mixer bowl.

2 With the flat beater on speed 4, gradually add the olive oil and then season with the salt and freshly ground black pepper.

3 Cut the garlic cloves in half and rub the cut ends over one side of each bread slice. Spread the tomato paste on top of the bread, then cook under a preheated broiler for 1 to 2 minutes or until warm. Serve immediately.

BLINIS Little Russian pancakes made from buckwheat flour that have become synonymous with cocktails and caviar. Alternative toppings include

a spoon of sour cream with some chives, smoked salmon, or salmon roe.

SERVES 6

Preparation time: 40 minutes plus

1 hour 30 minutes standing time

Cooking time: 35 minutes

Attachments used

1 cup milk

1¼ cups buckwheat flour

1 heaping teaspoon active dry yeast

1²/₃ cups all-purpose flour

1 egg, separated

2 tsp salt

1 cup sour cream

1 Warm the milk in a small saucepan to just below boiling. Put the buckwheat flour and yeast in the mixer bowl. Using the dough hook, on speed 4, add half of the milk to the flour mixture until well combined. Cover and leave to stand at room temperature for 1 hour until the mixture has doubled in volume.

2 Add the all-purpose flour, egg yolk, salt, sour cream, and the remaining milk to the bowl. Change to the flat beater and mix well on speed 4 until the mixture is smooth. Allow the mixture to stand for a further 30 minutes. Transfer to another bowl.

3 Clean the mixer bowl and dry thoroughly, then whisk the egg whites using the wire whip on speed 8 until peaking. Fold the egg whites into the batter carefully.

4 Heat two blini pans or one heavy-based skillet over a low heat for 7 minutes before using. Lightly grease the pans and spoon in enough batter to make a blini of ¼-inch thickness. Cook over a gentle heat for 2 to 3 minutes until browned on the underside, flip the blini over, and cook for a further minute. Remove from the pan and keep the blinis warm while repeating the cooking process with the remaining batter. Serve hot.

TAPENADE CROSTINI
Another Tuscan specialty, these thin slices of toast are topped with an olive paste made with anchovies and capers. Crostini can also be served with chicken livers, bell peppers, or eggplants.

SERVES 4 TO 6

Preparation time: 5 minutes

³/₄ cup black olives, pitted

2-oz can anchovy fillets, drained thoroughly

1 Tbsp capers

2 cloves garlic

2 Tbsp shredded fresh basil

About ³/₄ cup extra-virgin olive oil

1 large ciabatta loaf or other loaf, sliced

2 Tbsp shredded fresh basil, to garnish

Attachments used

1 Using the food grinder fitted with the fine grinding plate, on speed 4, shred the black olives, anchovy fillets, capers, and garlic into the mixer bowl and add 2 tablespoons shredded basil leaves.

2 With the flat beater on speed 4, gradually pour in just enough olive oil for the mixture to form a spreadable consistency. Scrape into a bowl, cover lightly, and store in the refrigerator until required.

3 Lightly toast the bread on both sides until crisp, top with the black olive paste, scatter over a few shredded basil leaves, and serve immediately.

COUNTRY PORK PÂTÉ
The olives in this country-style pâté could be replaced with mushrooms, while chorizo or salami can be added for extra flavor. The pâté can be frozen for up to a month.

SERVES 6 TO 8

Preparation time: 20 minutes,
   plus 1 to 2 days chilling

Cooking time: 2 hours

Attachments used

3 shallots

2–4 cloves garlic

2 Tbsp butter

1-lb piece pork belly, rind and bones removed (ask your butcher)

6 oz veal or pork fillet

6 oz chicken livers

5-oz piece prosciutto or pancetta

$1/3$ cup pitted black olives

5 Tbsp chopped fresh mixed herbs (thyme, parsley, basil)

2–3 Tbsp brandy

Salt and freshly ground black pepper

8–10 slices rindless lean bacon

1. Preheat the oven to 325ºF. Using the Rotor Slicer/Shredder, with the medium shredding cone attached, on speed 4, chop the shallots and garlic. Heat the butter in a skillet and sauté the shallot mixture for 5 minutes or until softened. Leave until cool.

2. Change to the food grinder and, with the fine grinding plate, on speed 4, shred the belly of pork, veal or pork fillet, the chicken livers, and prosciutto into a bowl. Chop the olives roughly. Add the remaining ingredients, except for the bacon, and mix together using the flat beater.

3. Line a 5-cup terrine dish with the bacon, leaving the ends so that they hang over the sides. Place the meat mixture into the dish and pack down firmly. Fold the bacon over the top and cover with either a lid or a double sheet of aluminum foil.

4. Place in a roasting pan half-filled with hot water. Cook in the oven for 1 hour 45 minutes to 2 hours or until the pâté has begun to shrink away from the sides of the dish and a skewer inserted into the center comes out clean.

The easiest way to grind raw meat or fish is to chill or partially freeze it to prevent any getting caught in the food grinder. Cutting away gristle and sinew also stops the meat becoming entangled in the knife or grinding plate.

5. Remove from the roasting pan and leave to cool for about an hour. Uncover the terrine dish, cover with clean foil, and weigh down with either clean weights or cans. Leave to cool completely, then place in the refrigerator.

6. Store the pâté in the refrigerator for 1 to 2 days before serving, keeping the weights in place, then eat within 2 to 3 days. Before serving, take the pâté out to return to room temperature for 30 minutes.

MAYONNAISE
One of the most versatile of French sauces, mayonnaise can be used as a summer dressing for vegetables and eggs, with fresh seafood, meats, or for dipping fries. This version is made with a whole egg and is very easy to do.

MAKES 1 CUP

Preparation time: 15 minutes

1 egg

1 egg yolk

1 tsp white wine vinegar or lemon juice

1 tsp Dijon mustard

1 cup olive oil

Salt and freshly ground black pepper

Attachments used

1   Warm the mixer bowl and wire whip with hot water, then dry thoroughly. Make sure all the ingredients are at room temperature.

2   Place the egg, egg yolk, vinegar or lemon juice, and mustard in the mixer bowl, attach the wire whip, and whisk, at speed 10, until well combined and frothy.

3   Add the oil very gradually, drop by drop at first, then more steadily as the mixture starts to thicken.

4   When all of the oil has been absorbed, season with the salt and black pepper, and add extra vinegar or lemon juice if required. The mixture should be very thick and stiff.

AÏOLI
A summery Provençal dish of garlic mayonnaise, which is usually eaten with fresh vegetables, but can also be served with a salad, eggs, poached fish, or a cold chicken. By leaving out the garlic, you can also use this recipe to make a rich, yolk-only mayonnaise.

MAKES 2¹/₂ CUPS

Preparation time: 10 minutes

5 cloves garlic

Pinch of salt

3 egg yolks

2 cups olive oil

1 Tbsp lemon juice

Attachments used

1   Finely chop the garlic and put into a pestle and mortar with the salt. Pound until smooth.

2   Warm the mixer bowl and wire whip with hot water, then dry thoroughly. Make sure all the ingredients are at room temperature.

3   Place the egg yolks and garlic in the mixer bowl and, with the wire whip, whisk on speed 6 for 1 minute until creamy.

4   Reducing the speed to speed 4, very slowly add the oil, drop by drop at first, ensuring each addition is fully incorporated before adding more, then gradually begin to add in a slow stream once the mixture is glossy and starts to thicken.

5   When all the oil has been absorbed, add the lemon juice if the mixture seems too thick.

CELERIAC REMOULADE
This classic French dish is made from the winter root vegetable celeriac, a type of celery that can be eaten raw or cooked, but is most famously used in this creamy salad.

SERVES 4

Preparation time: 20 minutes

Attachments used

1 Tbsp mustard

5 Tbsp vegetable oil

Juice of 1 lemon

1 Tbsp vinegar

1 Tbsp sour cream

Salt and freshly ground black pepper

1 lb celeriac

Small lettuce leaves, to garnish

1 Place the mustard, oil, and lemon juice in the mixer bowl and, using the wire whip, whisk together on speed 10. Add the vinegar and sour cream, season, then mix together again.

2 Peel the celeriac with a sharp knife and chop it into pieces. Using the Rotor Slicer/Shredder, fitted with the medium shredding cone, on speed 4, grate the celeriac and toss it in the sauce immediately, to prevent it discoloring. Garnish the remoulade with lettuce leaves and serve.

WHITE CABBAGE AND APPLE SALAD
A creamy German cabbage salad that marinates in a sour cream and white wine vinegar dressing overnight to produce a delicious salad that can be served with cheese and bread or sausage.

SERVES 6

Preparation time: 10 minutes plus overnight standing time

Attachments used

1 small white cabbage
1–2 shallots, peeled
3 small dessert apples, peeled and cored
Salt and freshly ground black pepper
1 Tbsp white wine vinegar
4 Tbsp sour cream
2 Tbsp walnut halves

1 Remove the outer leaves and hard inner core of the cabbage and cut into wedges. Cut the shallots in half.

2 Using the Rotor Slicer/Shredder, with the coarse shredding cone attached, on speed 4, shred the cabbage, shallots, and apples into the mixer bowl. Add seasoning to taste and, using the flat beater, stir until well mixed.

3 Blend the vinegar and sour cream together and pour over the cabbage, mix well, cover, and store in the refrigerator overnight.

4 When ready to serve, use the Rotor Slicer/Shredder, with the coarse shredding cone attached, on speed 4, to chop the walnuts. Spoon the cabbage salad into a serving bowl and sprinkle with the nuts.

RED CABBAGE SALAD
This attractive German red cabbage salad goes well with both hot and cold foods.

To turn it into a light lunch dish, chop and add some cooked bratwurst sausage or ham.

SERVES 6

Preparation time: 15 minutes

¹/₂ small red cabbage (about 1 lb)

2 carrots, peeled

1 white onion

2 green dessert apples

2 Tbsp lemon juice

3 oz baby corn, halved lengthwise

¹/₃ cup dried cranberries (optional)

For the dressing

4 Tbsp sour cream

1 tsp German or English mustard

1 tsp sugar

2 Tbsp white wine vinegar

Salt and freshly ground black pepper

¹/₂–1 tsp caraway seeds

Attachments used

1 Remove the outer leaves and hard central core from the cabbage. With the slicing cone on the Rotor Slicer/Shredder, on speed 4, slice the red cabbage into a colander. Rinse well under cold water until the water runs clear. Drain thoroughly then place in the mixer bowl.

2 With the coarse shredding cone on the Rotor Slicer/Shredder, on speed 4, shred the carrots and the onion into the mixer bowl.

3 Core the apple, peel if preferred, then coarsely shred, on speed 4, into a small bowl. Add the lemon juice and toss well, then stir into the red cabbage mixture.

4 Blanch the baby corn in a pan of salted boiling water for 3 minutes, drain, and add to the cabbage, together with the dried cranberries, if using. Mix lightly together.

5 To make the dressing, place all the ingredients in the mixer bowl and, using the flat beater on speed 2, blend together, then pour over the cabbage. Toss everything lightly together and serve.

ICED ZUCCHINI SOUP WITH SAGE This chilled summer soup makes a beautiful appetizer or a

light lunch. You could replace the Parmesan with old Edam cheese and use nut oil instead of olive oil.

SERVES 4

Preparation time: 10 minutes

Cooking time: 10 minutes

2 zucchini

2 oz Parmesan cheese

2 Tbsp olive oil

2 ice cubes

Salt and freshly ground black pepper

16 sage leaves

1¹/₂ Tbsp oil, for frying

Cayenne pepper (optional)

Attachments used

Blender used

1 Attach the slicing cone to the Rotor Slicer/Shredder and slice the zucchini. Cook in a pan of salted boiling water for 5 minutes. Drain the slices and leave to cool. Shave the Parmesan into thin slices.

2 In the blender, mix the zucchini on stir speed with the olive oil, ice cubes, four pinches of salt, and freshly ground black pepper until liquefied.

3 Rinse and pat dry the sage leaves. Heat the remaining oil in a skillet, add the leaves, and fry for 1 minute, then drain them on paper towels. Keep four leaves aside.

4 Chop the other 12 sage leaves and stir into the zucchini mixture. Pour into four bowls. Garnish each with a sage leaf and some Parmesan flakes, and dust with cayenne pepper if desired.

PEA SOUP
Pea soups are a favorite wintertime dish in Holland and Belgium and this one is a meal in itself, with croûtons of bread, golden fried onions, and crispy bacon pieces added just before serving.

SERVES 4 TO 6

Preparation time: 20 minutes

Cooking time: 20 minutes

Attachments used

5^1/$_2$ cups frozen peas, thawed

5 cups chicken or vegetable broth

Salt and freshly ground black pepper

1 tsp dried marjoram

2 Tbsp chopped fresh parsley

4 Tbsp light cream (optional)

8 oz lean bacon slices

1 large onion

3 Tbsp butter

5 slices white bread

1 Using the food grinder fitted with the fine grinding plate, on speed 4, grind the peas. Place in a saucepan, add the broth, bring to a boil, then add a little seasoning with the dried marjoram. Cover with a lid, reduce the heat, and simmer for 15 minutes or until really soft.

2 Pass the peas with their liquid through the strainer, on speed 4, return to the rinsed pan, adjust the seasoning, and add the chopped parsley. Heat through until hot and keep warm. Just before serving, stir in the cream.

3 Meanwhile attach the Rotor Slicer/Shredder with the coarse shredding cone attached, on speed 4, and pass the bacon through and then the onion separately.

4 Heat half of the butter and sauté the bacon until crisp, remove with a slotted draining spoon, and reserve. Add the onion to the butter remaining in the pan and fry until softened. Drain well.

5 Discard the crusts from the bread and cut into small cubes. Heat the remaining butter in a skillet and sauté the cubes for 5 minutes, stirring frequently, or until crisp and golden.

6 Mix the bacon, onion, and croûtons together and serve with the soup.

POTATO SOUP

Hearty country-style potato soups are a mainstay of the European winter. This version is made with celery, carrot, and leek, and can be garnished with bacon, croûtons, and green onions or a swirl of sour cream and chives.

SERVES 4

Preparation time: 15 minutes

Cooking time: 45 minutes

Attachments used

2 lb potatoes, cut into wedges

4 celery stalks

1 carrot

1 leek, trimmed and washed well

1 onion, sliced

1 stick butter

1¼ cups water

Salt and freshly ground black pepper

1¼ cups cream

¼ tsp freshly grated nutmeg, or to taste

Croûtons, to garnish

Crispy fried chopped bacon, to garnish

Diagonally sliced green onions, to garnish

1 Using the Rotor Slicer/Shredder, with the slicing cone attached, on speed 4, slice the potatoes into the mixer bowl, then remove them to a large saucepan. Still on speed 4, slice the celery, carrot, leek, and onion separately.

2 Add half of the butter to the saucepan and place over a gentle heat. Cook gently, stirring frequently until the potatoes are coated in the butter. Add the celery and carrot, and cook for a further 2 minutes, stirring.

3 Pour in the water, add seasoning, and bring to a boil. Cover and simmer for 20 to 25 minutes, or until the potatoes are really tender.

4 Attach the strainer and, on speed 4, pass half the soup through the strainer and return to a clean saucepan. Stir in the remaining unpuréed soup.

5 Melt the remaining butter, and sauté the leek and onion for 5 to 8 minutes or until softened, then stir the leek mixture, together with any butter remaining in the pan, into the soup. Stir in the cream with the nutmeg and heat gently, stirring, and taking care not to allow the soup to boil. Adjust the seasoning and serve garnished with croûtons, crispy bacon, and sliced green onions.

ONION SOUP GRATINÉE

This version of the French bistro classic is made with coarsely sliced onions, cooked slowly, then heated under the broiler to let the Gruyère melt over the toasted bread and soup.

SERVES 4

Preparation time: 40 minutes

Cooking time: 10 minutes

Attachments used

4 oz Gruyère cheese

3 onions

4 large slices baguette

1 Tbsp butter

1 Tbsp all-purpose flour

5 cups warm water

Salt and freshly ground black pepper

2 tsp fresh chives

1 Using the Rotor Slicer/Shredder with the medium shredding cone attached, on speed 4, shred the cheese. Change to the slicing cone and slice the onions, on speed 4. Toast the bread in an oven or in a skillet.

2 In a casserole, sauté the sliced onions in the butter over a low heat, stirring occasionally, for about 25 minutes. Dust the onions with the flour and continue to sauté until golden brown, stirring constantly. Add the warm water, mix well, and leave to cook for 10 minutes.

3 Add three-quarters of the cheese to the casserole. Season with salt and pepper and stir in the chives.

4 Pour the soup into individual soup bowls or a large tureen. Top with the toasted slices of bread and sprinkle with the remaining cheese. Place briefly under a preheated broiler to melt the cheese, then serve immediately.

GAZPACHO
A classic summer soup from Spain that tastes best when made with ripe and flavorful Mediterranean tomatoes and vegetables and Spanish olive oil. Add the ice cubes and serve it very cold.

SERVES 4 TO 6

Preparation time: 15 minutes plus at least 1 hour chilling time

Attachments used

1½ lb ripe tomatoes, cores removed

1 red bell pepper, deseeded

1 green bell pepper, deseeded

1 red onion

½ cucumber, deseeded

2 cloves garlic, finely chopped

1 Tbsp finely chopped fresh parsley

1 Tbsp finely chopped fresh basil leaves

1½ Tbsp red wine vinegar

½ cup puréed tomatoes

⅓ cup water

3 drops Tabasco

4 Tbsp olive oil

Salt and freshly ground black pepper

Cubes of frozen olive oil and fresh basil leaves, to serve

1 Using the Rotor Slicer/Shredder with the slicing cone attached, on speed 4, coarsely shred all the vegetables into the mixer bowl.

2 Add all the other ingredients and mix thoroughly with the flat beater on speed 4, seasoning well with salt and pepper. Refrigerate for 12 hours if possible, to allow the flavors to mellow and blend.

3 Serve this soup with cubes of frozen olive oil and some fresh basil leaves.

MINESTRONE WITH PESTO
A thick Italian vegetable soup, which can be served as a main meal with some bread. The borlotti beans in the recipe can be replaced with either haricot or kidney beans.

SERVES 4 TO 6

Preparation time: 20 minutes plus overnight soaking if using dried beans

Attachments used

Cooking time: 1 hour

1 cup dried borlotti beans, or 1^2/$_3$ cups canned, rinsed and drained

4 small potatoes, peeled

2 carrots

2 small leeks

2 celery stalks

2 small zucchini

1 onion

5^1/$_2$ cups water

4 Tbsp olive oil, plus extra to serve

2 medium tomatoes, skinned, deseeded, and roughly chopped

2 oz green herbs, such as sorrel, chervil, or parsley

1 cup shortcut macaroni

2 Tbsp pesto (see page 36)

Salt and freshly ground black pepper

Freshly grated Parmesan cheese, to serve

1 If using dried beans, rinse them well, then cover with plenty of cold water and leave overnight. Drain well, then place the beans in a saucepan, and cover with water. Bring to a boil, then drain and cover again with cold water. Return to boiling and simmer for 15 minutes, then drain and reserve.

2 Using the Rotor Slicer/Shredder, fitted with the slicing cone, on speed 4, slice all the vegetables, except the tomatoes, into the mixer bowl.

3 Bring the water to a boil, add the beans – if using dried – and the prepared vegetables. Stir in the olive oil, return to boiling, then cover the pan and simmer for 30 minutes.

4 Add the tomatoes and the green herbs to the soup, together with the canned beans if using. Cook for a further 15 minutes.

5 About 5 minutes before the end of the cooking time, add the pasta to the soup. Cook until firm to the bite, *al dente*.

6 Mix the pesto with a ladleful of the hot soup, then stir into the rest of the soup with seasoning to taste. Serve immediately, with extra olive oil and black pepper, and sprinkled with the Parmesan cheese. Decorate with green herbs.

RED BELL PEPPER AND CHILI SOUP
For a dramatic effect, make two batches of this Mexican-style soup, using red bell peppers in one and yellow bell peppers in the other. To serve, ladle the red pepper soup into shallow soup bowls, then ladle some of the yellow pepper into the center to form a "sunburst."

SERVES 4

Preparation time: 15 minutes

Cooking time: 30 minutes

Blender used

2 Tbsp olive oil

1 onion, roughly chopped

1–3 cloves garlic, sliced

1 red chili, deseeded and chopped

4 red bell peppers, skinned, deseeded, and sliced

3 tomatoes, skinned and deseeded

3³/₄ cups vegetable or chicken broth

Salt and freshly ground black pepper

Sour cream and snipped fresh chives, to garnish

1 Heat the oil in a large pan and sauté the onion, garlic, and chili for 5 minutes, stirring frequently. Add the peppers and continue to sauté for a further 2 minutes. Stir in the tomatoes together with the broth and a little seasoning, and bring to a boil.

2 Cover with a lid, reduce the heat, and simmer for 20 minutes, or until the peppers are really soft. Remove from the heat and allow to cool. Place in the blender and mix on purée speed until the mixture is well combined. If you want a really smooth soup, rub the purée through a fine strainer. Return the soup to the pan, adjust the seasoning, and reheat gently.

3 Pour into warmed soup bowls. Swirl the soup with sour cream and sprinkle with the chives. Serve with fresh bread.

PIZZA, PASTA, GNOCCHI, AND NOODLES

PIZZA MARGHERITA
One of Italy's original pizzas, created in Naples to honor the visiting Queen Margherita. This recipe makes enough for two pizzas – if you only want to make one, freeze one portion of the dough and cut the topping ingredients in half.

MAKES 2 PIZZAS

Preparation time: 10 minutes plus standing time

Cooking time: 15 to 20 minutes

Attachments used

3 cups white bread flour

$1/2$ tsp salt

1 heaping tsp active dry yeast

2 Tbsp olive oil

$1^{1}/3$ cups tepid water

For the toppings

Two 14-oz cans chopped or whole tomatoes, mashed and drained

10 oz mozzarella cheese, thinly sliced

Olive oil

Salt

Two handfuls of fresh basil

1   Preheat the oven to 425°F. Place the flour, salt, and yeast into the mixer bowl. Using the flat beater, on speed 2, mix the dry ingredients together for a few seconds.

2   Change to the dough hook and, on speed 2, add the olive oil, then gradually add the water and begin to knead. If the dough looks at all dry, add a little more water until the mixture looks moist. Knead for about 1 minute only on this speed.

3   Cover with the plastic bowl cover and leave to rise in a warm, draft-free place for about 1 hour, or until doubled in bulk.

4   Knead well again, adding a little extra flour if the dough seems too sticky. The machine may be stopped once or twice and the dough pulled away from hook.

5   Divide the dough in two and roll out into thin circles. Grease two cookie sheets.

6   Put the tomatoes on first with your fingers or a fork, trying not to make the dough too wet. Add the slices of mozzarella, then a drizzle of olive oil, some salt, and the basil. Bake in the oven for 15 to 20 minutes until golden.

VARIATIONS

MUSHROOM AND PARMA HAM PIZZA – Sauté a chopped onion, 2–3 minced cloves garlic and 3 cups assorted sliced mushrooms for 5 minutes, then add a 14-oz can chopped tomatoes and simmer for another 5 minutes. Drain thoroughly and spread over one of the pizza bases. Top with 4 oz Parma ham strips and 1 cup sliced mozzarella. Bake, then serve sprinkled with some shredded basil.

SPINACH AND GOAT CHEESE PIZZA – Sauté a chopped onion and 2–3 minced cloves garlic for 3 minutes. Add a deseeded and sliced yellow bell pepper and 2 sliced tomatoes to the pan and cook for a further 3 minutes. Drain thoroughly, then mix with 5 oz thawed and well-drained frozen spinach, $1/4$ tsp fresh grated nutmeg, and some seasoning. Spread this mixture over one of the pizza bases and top with 1 Tbsp chopped fresh oregano and 4 oz crumbled goat cheese before baking.

PASTA SAUCES

These are the four classic Italian sauces, which can be used to make lasagnes or cannelloni. They are all wonderful on their own, served with homemade pasta. The béchamel sauce can also be used in place of a simple roux.

BÉCHAMEL SAUCE

This French white sauce is flavored with vegetables and can be used as a topping for lasagne or cannelloni, or to bind together a pasta sauce or vegetable gratin.

MAKES 1¹/₄ CUPS

Preparation time: 10 minutes plus 15 minutes infusing time

Cooking time: 10 minutes

Attachments used

1 small onion, cut into wedges

1 small carrot, cut into chunks

1 celery stalk

1 bay leaf

1¹/₄ cups milk

1 blade mace

3 Tbsp butter

¹/₃ cup all-purpose flour

Salt and freshly ground black pepper

1–2 Tbsp light cream (optional)

1 Using the Rotor Slicer/Shredder, with the slicing cone attached, on speed 4, slice the vegetables into the mixer bowl, then place them in a heavy-base saucepan. Add the bay leaf and the milk with the mace.

2 Place over a gentle heat and warm until almost boiling, then remove, cover with a lid, and leave to infuse for 15 minutes, or longer if time permits. Strain and discard the vegetables and herbs.

3 Melt the butter in a heavy-base saucepan, then sprinkle in the flour, and cook over a gentle heat for 2 minutes, stirring throughout. Take off the heat, then gradually stir in the strained milk.

4 Return to the heat and cook, stirring, until the sauce thickens and coats the back of a wooden spoon. Remove from the heat and add seasoning to taste, and the cream if using.

PESTO

This fresh Italian sauce from Genoa makes a great marinade for broiled chicken or fish, or it can be stirred into homemade pasta; a spoonful added to a bowl of vegetable soup; or drizzled over a mozzarella and tomato salad.

MAKES ³/₄ CUP

Preparation time: 15 minutes

Attachments used

Blender used

2 oz Parmesan or Pecorino cheese

1 oz fresh basil leaves

¹/₂ cup toasted pine nuts

²/₃ cup extra-virgin olive oil

Freshly ground black pepper

1 Using a grater, or attaching the fine shredding cone to the Rotor Slicer/Shredder, on speed 4, shred the Parmesan cheese.

2 Place the basil leaves and pine nuts in the blender and blend at stir speed until chopped fine. Then, with the motor running, slowly pour in the olive oil, drop by drop. When about half the oil has been added, you can gradually start to add bigger amounts of oil, until it has all been used.

3 Scrape the mixture into a bowl, stir in the shredded Parmesan, and season to taste with the pepper. Store any excess, covered, in the refrigerator.

TOMATO PASSATA
This basic Italian cooked tomato passata can be eaten on its own with pasta, a little basil, and Parmesan, or added to pasta sauces, stews, or used on pizza bases. Try to find very ripe tomatoes with lots of flavor.

SERVES 4

Preparation time: 5 minutes
Cooking time: 45 minutes

2 lb fresh tomatoes, quartered
1 onion
1 celery stalk
1 carrot
2 Tbsp olive oil
Salt and freshly ground black pepper

Attachments used

1 Using the fruit/vegetable strainer, on speed 4, process the tomatoes into a saucepan.

2 Attach the fine shredding cone and shred the onion, celery, and carrot. Heat the oil and sauté the grated vegetables until soft. Add to the saucepan with the tomatoes. Season and bring to a boil. Simmer for 40 minutes until a thick sauce is obtained.

BOLOGNESE SAUCE
An authentic Italian Bolognese sauce, made with your own ground steak and pork to ensure that the meat is very tender. Spinach tagliatelle also goes really well with this.

SERVES 4

Preparation time: 30 minutes
Cooking time: 40 minutes

1 celery stalk, trimmed
1 onion
1 large carrot
10 oz lean beef (round steak, sirloin, or blade)
3 oz pork
1 Tbsp butter or olive oil
6 medium ripe tomatoes, peeled and chopped
1 Tbsp tomato paste
2/3 cup beef broth
Salt and freshly ground black pepper
1 bay leaf (optional)
Freshly grated Parmesan cheese

Attachments used

1 Cut the vegetables into chunks and using the food grinder, fitted with the coarse grinding plate, on speed 4, grind into the mixer bowl. Cut the beef and pork into strips and feed through the food grinder into the bowl.

2 Heat the butter or oil in a large saucepan and sauté the vegetables and meat for 5 to 8 minutes, stirring frequently until the meat is turning brown.

3 Cook for 2 minutes, then add the tomatoes and tomato paste, and gradually stir in the broth. Add seasoning to taste, and the bay leaf if using, and bring to a boil. Cover with a lid, reduce the heat, and simmer for 30 minutes. Adjust the seasoning and serve with tagliatelle and Parmesan cheese.

BASIC PASTA DOUGH

This pasta dough recipe can be used to make any of the recipes in this book. Simply cut the rolled-out dough into sheets for lasagne and ravioli, or pass through the cutters to make tagliatelle or linguine.

MAKES 1 LB PASTA DOUGH

Preparation time: 10 minutes plus 1 hour chilling time

Attachments used

2³⁄₄ cups 00 flour, durum wheat flour, or all-purpose flour

3 medium eggs

1 Tbsp olive oil

1 Place the flour, eggs, and oil in the mixer bowl and attach the flat beater. On speed 1, mix slowly until the mixture is thoroughly combined. Exchange the flat beater for the dough hook and gradually increase the speed to 4, kneading for 5 to 8 minutes until a smooth, elastic pasta dough is formed. Wrap in plastic wrap and leave to chill in the refrigerator for at least 1 hour.

2 Attach the pasta roller to the mixer and adjust to setting 1. Cut the dough into eight pieces and pass one portion very slowly through the roller at speed 2, then fold it in half. Do this four to five times. When the dough is no longer sticky, adjust to setting 2 and pass the pasta through, but do not fold the dough this time. Continue rolling the dough through four to five times on each setting until the desired setting is reached. Repeat with the other portions of dough. The pasta dough is now ready to be cut.

VARIATIONS

SPINACH PASTA – Instead of one of the eggs, add ¹⁄₄ cup cooked, very well-drained and chopped spinach to the mixer bowl.

BLACK INK PASTA – Add 1 teaspoon of squid ink to the mixer bowl with the rest of the ingredients.

RED BEET PASTA – In the blender, on purée speed, process 1 oz fresh cooked beet until really smooth. Add to the mixer bowl with the rest of the ingredients. For a deeper color, add another 1 oz beet.

LINGUINE WITH GARLIC, OIL, AND CHILI
This classic Italian sauce is so simple it allows you to appreciate the flavor and texture of the strands of very fine homemade linguine.

SERVES 4

Preparation time: 20 minutes

Cooking time: 10 minutes

Attachments used

1 quantity basic pasta dough (page 38), rolled out to a setting 6 to 8 thickness

For the sauce
6–8 Tbsp extra-virgin olive oil
2–4 cloves garlic, finely chopped
1/2 tsp dried chili flakes
Salt and freshly ground black pepper
Freshly shaved Parmesan cheese
2–3 Tbsp chopped fresh flat-leaf parsley

1 Attach the linguine fini cutter to the pasta maker and feed through the sheets of pasta dough on speed 2, cutting the strands to a spaghetti-length with scissors as they come through. Lay in a single layer on a clean dish towel or over a pasta drying rack if cooking immediately. If you want to use the pasta more than an hour after cutting it, toss it in a little flour to keep the linguine from sticking together, and wrap the strands round to form nests. Leave on a dish towel to dry, then store in an airtight tin.

2 Heat the oil in a heavy-base pan and add the garlic and chili flakes, cook gently for 5 minutes, then add the seasoning. Remove from the heat and cover with a lid.

3 Cook the linguine in plenty of lightly salted boiling water for 1 to 2 minutes or until tender to the bite, *al dente*. Drain and return to the pan, then add the garlic/chili-infused oil, and heat through for 1 to 2 minutes, tossing lightly until the pasta is evenly coated with the flavored oil. Sprinkle with the shaved Parmesan and chopped parsley. Serve with plenty of warm bread.

TAGLIATELLE WITH PARMESAN AND CILANTRO SAUCE

This speckled tagliatelle is slightly spicy and is served with a simple cilantro pesto made with lots of Parmesan cheese.

SERVES 4 TO 6

Preparation time: 20 minutes plus

1 hour chilling time

Cooking time: 3 minutes

Attachments used

Blender used

4 cups 00, durum wheat or all-purpose flour

5 medium eggs

1 tsp turmeric

1 tsp paprika

1 Tbsp black pepper

For the Parmesan and cilantro sauce

5 oz Parmesan cheese, shredded

2 Tbsp fresh cilantro

2 Tbsp pine nuts

Sea salt

2 Tbsp olive oil

1 Place the flour, eggs, turmeric, paprika, and black pepper in the mixer bowl and attach the flat beater. On speed 1, mix slowly until the mixture is thoroughly combined. Exchange the flat beater for the dough hook and gradually increase the speed to 4, kneading for 5 to 8 minutes until a smooth, elastic pasta dough is formed. Wrap in plastic wrap and leave to chill in the refrigerator for at least 1 hour.

2 Attach the pasta roller to the mixer and adjust to setting 1. Cut the dough into eight pieces and pass one portion very slowly through the roller at speed 2, then fold it in half. Do this four to five times. When the dough is no longer sticky, adjust to setting 2 and pass the pasta through, but do not fold the dough this time. Continue rolling the dough through four to five times on each setting until setting 5 is reached. Repeat with the other portions of dough.

3 Attach the fettuccine tagliatelle cutter to the pasta maker and feed through the sheets of pasta dough on speed 2, cutting the strands to a spaghetti-length with scissors as they come through. Lay in a single layer on a clean dish towel or over a pasta drying rack if cooking immediately. If you want to use the pasta more than an hour after cutting

it, toss it in a little flour to keep the tagliatelle from sticking together and wrap the strands round to form nests. Leave on a dish towel to dry, then store in an airtight tin.

4 Using a mortar and pestle or the blender, process the Parmesan, cilantro leaves, pine nuts, a little sea salt, and the olive oil at stir speed ⊛ until well combined.

5 Cook the tagliatelle in plenty of lightly salted boiling water for 3 minutes or until tender to the bite, *al dente*. Drain, mix with the Parmesan and cilantro sauce, and serve immediately.

EGGPLANT AND PARMESAN LASAGNE A classic lasagne dish, with the delicious Italian combination of ripe tomatoes, eggplants cooked in olive oil, and Parmesan and mozzarella cheeses.

To make the pasta dough easy to handle, divide it into manageable portions about the size of eggs, then flatten each piece out a little before feeding it slowly through the roller. While you roll and cut out each portion of dough, keep the rest of the portions covered with some plastic wrap to stop them drying out.

SERVES 4 TO 6

Preparation time: 30 minutes

Cooking time: 45 minutes

Attachments used

1 quantity basic pasta dough (page 38), rolled out to a setting 7 thickness

1 quantity tomato passata (page 37)

1 quantity béchamel sauce (page 36)

4 oz Parmesan cheese

6–8 Tbsp extra-virgin olive oil

2 eggplants, chopped

12 oz mozzarella cheese, diced

1 Preheat the oven to 425°F. Lay the sheets of rolled-out pasta onto a floured surface and cut into rectangular sheets, about 6 x 3 inches.

2 Bring a large saucepan of lightly salted water to a boil and cook two to three sheets of pasta for 1 minute, then plunge into cold water that has had a little olive oil added. Drain well on clean dish towels and reserve. Repeat until all the pasta sheets have been blanched. Cover with clean dish towels to prevent the pasta from drying out.

3 Attach the fine shredding cone to the Rotor Slicer/Shredder and, on speed 4, shred the Parmesan cheese.

4 Stir the tomato sauce and one-third of the béchamel sauce together, then stir in half of the grated Parmesan cheese.

5 Heat 4 tablespoons of the olive oil and gently sauté the eggplant for 10 minutes or until tender, stirring frequently. Add more oil as necessary to prevent the eggplant sticking to the pan.

6 Place a layer of lasagne sheets in the base of a large greased gratin dish. Spoon over the tomato sauce mixture, sprinkle over the mozzarella, and then the eggplant. Cover with the remaining lasagne sheets, spoon over the remaining béchamel sauce, and sprinkle with the remaining Parmesan cheese. Bake in the oven for 20 to 25 minutes or until golden brown and bubbly, and thoroughly heated through.

PEPPERS AND BROCCOLI LASAGNE A vegetarian lasagne, this dish is hearty, with

cannellini beans making up the sauce along with fresh vegetables. Instead of a tomato sauce, it is topped with slices of fresh tomato.

SERVES 4 TO 6

Preparation time: 30 minutes

Cooking time: 40 minutes

Attachments used

1 quantity basic pasta dough (page 38), rolled out to a setting 7 thickness

1 quantity béchamel sauce (page 36)

2 carrots

1 red bell pepper, deseeded

1 yellow bell pepper, deseeded

6 oz broccoli

4 oz green beans, cut into small lengths

14-oz can cannellini beans, drained and rinsed

2 oz Parmesan cheese

4 firm tomatoes, sliced

3 medium eggs

1/2 cup thick yogurt

1 Preheat the oven to 375°F. Lay the sheets of rolled-out pasta onto a floured surface and cut into rectangular sheets, about 6 x 3 inches.

2 Bring a large saucepan of lightly salted water to a boil and cook two to three sheets of pasta for 1 minute, then plunge into cold water that has had a little olive oil added. Drain well on clean dish towels and reserve. Repeat until all the pasta sheets have been blanched. Cover with clean dish towels to prevent the pasta from drying out.

3 Using the Rotor Slicer/Shredder with the slicing cone attached, on speed 4, slice the carrots and peppers. Cut the broccoli into small flowerets, then plunge the broccoli into boiling water together with the green beans. Cook for 2 minutes, then drain and refresh in cold water. Drain again, and add to the carrots and peppers with the cannellini beans.

4 Changing to the fine shredding cone, still on speed 4, shred the Parmesan cheese.

5 Place half the béchamel sauce in the base of a lightly oiled gratin dish and top with half the vegetables. Cover with four lasagne sheets and repeat the layering, ending with the lasagne.

6 Arrange the tomato slices over the pasta. Beat the eggs and yogurt together, pour over the tomatoes, and sprinkle with the Parmesan. Bake in the oven for 25 to 30 minutes, or until golden brown and bubbly, and thoroughly heated through, then serve immediately.

CRAB AND GREEN ONION CANNELLONI
If you are fortunate enough to live in an area where freshly caught crabs are available, this recipe is a must for you. However, it is possible to use canned or frozen crab, but ensure that you squeeze out all the excess moisture.

SERVES 4 TO 6

Preparation time: 30 minutes

Cooking time: 35 minutes

Attachments used

1 quantity basic pasta dough (page 38), rolled out to a setting 6 thickness
1 quantity tomato passata (page 37)

6 green onions, trimmed and chopped
2–3 small jalapeño chilis, deseeded
3 firm tomatoes, peeled and deseeded
12 oz white crab meat
Salt and freshly ground black pepper
2 oz Gruyère cheese
Fresh parsley sprigs, to garnish

1 Preheat the oven to 375°F. Lay the sheets of rolled-out pasta onto a floured surface and cut into rectangular sheets, about 6 x 3 inches.

2 Bring a large saucepan of lightly salted water to a boil and cook two to three sheets of pasta for 1 minute, then plunge into cold water that has had a little olive oil added. Drain well on clean dish towels and reserve. Repeat until all the pasta sheets have been blanched. Cover with clean dish towels to prevent the pasta from drying out.

3 Using the Rotor Slicer/Shredder, fitted with the medium shredding cone, on speed 4, mince the green onions, chilis, and tomatoes into the mixer bowl. Add the crab meat, with seasoning to taste, and mix together.

4 Change to the fine shredding cone and, still on speed 4, shred the cheese.

5 Place about 2 tablespoons of the filling at one end of a lasagne sheet. Moisten the edges and roll up to encase the filling. Place the filled tubes, seam-side down, into the base of a greased ovenproof dish. Pour over the tomato sauce, sprinkle with the cheese, then bake in the oven for 25 minutes or until golden and bubbly. Garnish with the parsley sprigs.

SPINACH, MUSHROOM, AND RICOTTA CANNELLONI

Sheets of homemade fresh pasta are quick to roll up into great cannelloni tubes. This spinach, mushroom, and ricotta filling would work equally well in ravioli or lasagne.

SERVES 4 TO 6

Preparation time: 30 minutes

Cooking time: 35 minutes

Attachments used

1 quantity basic pasta dough (page 38), rolled out to a setting 6 thickness

1 quantity tomato passata (page 37)

1 Tbsp olive oil

1 small onion, chopped

3 oz mushrooms, chopped fine

1 cup ricotta cheese

1 cup frozen spinach, thawed

$1/4$–$1/2$ tsp freshly grated nutmeg

Salt and freshly ground black pepper

2 oz mozzarella cheese

1 Preheat the oven to 375ºF. Lay the sheets of rolled-out pasta onto a floured surface and cut into rectangular sheets, about 6 x 3 inches.

2 Bring a large saucepan of lightly salted water to a boil and cook two to three sheets of pasta for 1 minute, then plunge into cold water that has had a little olive oil added. Drain well on clean dish towels and reserve. Repeat until all the pasta sheets have been blanched. Cover with clean dish towels to prevent the pasta from drying out.

3 Heat the oil in a small pan and sauté the onion and mushrooms for 5 minutes. Drain and reserve.

4 With the flat beater on speed 4, beat the ricotta cheese in the mixer bowl until soft and creamy, then beat in the onion mixture. Squeeze out any excess moisture from the spinach and beat into the cheese, with the nutmeg and seasoning to taste.

5 Using the Rotor Slicer/Shredder, fitted with the fine shredding cone, on speed 4, shred the mozzarella cheese.

6 Place about 2 tablespoons of the filling at one end of a lasagne sheet. Moisten the edges and roll up to encase the filling. Place the filled tubes, seam-side down, into the base of a greased ovenproof dish. Pour over the tomato sauce and sprinkle with the mozzarella, then bake in the oven for 25 minutes or until golden and bubbly.

RAVIOLI

These fat squares of Italian fresh pasta are filled with a pork, red wine, and herb filling. Here they are served with a tomato sauce and Parmesan cheese, but you could just pour over melted butter and a handful of fresh chopped herbs.

SERVES 4 TO 6

Preparation time: 30 minutes plus
1 hour standing time

Cooking time: 40 minutes

Attachments used

1 quantity basic pasta dough (page 38), rolled out to a setting 6 thickness
1 quantity tomato passata (page 37)

1 onion
1 carrot
1 celery stalk
1 large clove garlic
4 oz lean pork or veal, trimmed and cut into chunks
4 oz prosciutto
1 Tbsp chopped fresh oregano leaves
Salt and freshly ground black pepper
1 Tbsp olive oil
3–4 Tbsp red wine or broth
2 oz Parmesan cheese
Flour, for dusting

1 Using the Rotor Slicer/Shredder, with the medium shredding cone attached, on speed 4, chop the onion, carrot, celery, and garlic into the mixer bowl.

2 Change to the food grinder, with the fine grinding plate attached, on speed 4, and grind the pork or veal and the prosciutto into the bowl with the vegetables. Add the oregano and seasoning to taste and mix well.

3 Heat the oil in a large pan and gently cook the meat and vegetables with the wine or broth for 20 to 30 minutes, or until cooked, stirring frequently, and taking care not to let the mixture dry out or burn. Remove, drain, and leave until cool.

4 Attach the fine shredding cone to the Rotor Slicer/Shredder and, on speed 4, shred the Parmesan.

5 Lay the sheets of rolled-out pasta onto a floured surface and cut into rectangular sheets, about 6 x 3 inches.

6 Place one strip of pasta on the lightly floured surface. Put the filling in a piping bag fitted with a large potato nozzle or use a teaspoon to place teaspoonfuls of the filling at 2-inch intervals on the pasta.

7 Moisten the edges of another piece of pasta and place it on top to encase the fillings. Sprinkle with a little flour and leave for about 1 hour. Repeat with the remaining pasta sheets and filling.

8 Using a pasta wheel or knife, cut at 2-inch intervals between the fillings to make squares. Cut along all the edges to give a fluted edge and pinch the edges firmly together.

9 Cook the ravioli in plenty of lightly salted boiling water for 3 to 4 minutes or until tender to the bite, *al dente*. Drain well then return to the pan, add the tomato sauce, and heat through. Serve immediately with Parmesan.

BEEF AND PORK POCKETS (Schwäbische Maultaschen) Little ravioli from the south of Germany, which are

usually served in a broth with a sprinkling of herbs as an appetizer, but can also be sprinkled with onion rings fried in a little butter until golden.

SERVES 4

Preparation time: 45 minutes plus 30 minutes

standing time

Cooking time: 20 minutes

Attachments used

1 quantity basic pasta dough (page 38), rolled out to a setting 6 to 7
    thickness

1 bread roll

8 oz good-quality beef, such as round or blade steak

2 oz smoked lean bacon

1 small onion

4 oz pork sausage meat

1 tsp butter

8 oz fresh spinach

1 Tbsp chopped fresh parsley

1 medium egg

Salt and freshly ground black pepper

1/2 tsp freshly grated nutmeg

5 cups beef broth

2 Tbsp snipped fresh chives

1 Cover the bread roll with cold water and reserve. Trim the beef and cut into strips. Using the food grinder, fitted with the fine grinding plate, on speed 4, grind the beef, bacon, and onion into the mixer bowl. Add the sausage meat and mix well with the flat beater on speed 2.

2 Heat the butter in a skillet and sauté the meat mixture for 5 minutes, stirring frequently until brown. Cover the spinach with boiling water, drain thoroughly, and squeeze out excess moisture. Squeeze out the moisture from the bread roll, then add the spinach, parsley, and bread roll to the meat mixture. Beat the egg, then add to the meat with seasoning to taste, and the nutmeg. Mix well with the flat beater on speed 2.

3 Lay the sheets of rolled-out pasta onto a floured surface and, using a 2-inch pastry cutter, cut the dough into rounds. Place a spoonful of the prepared filling in the center of each round, moisten the edge,s and fold over to form a semi-circle. Press the edges firmly together. Cover and leave to dry for 30 minutes.

4 Bring the beef broth to a boil, then drop a few of the filled pockets into the broth and cook gently for 10 to 15 minutes. Drain and keep warm while cooking the remaining pockets. When all the pockets are cooked, return to the hot broth and serve sprinkled with the chives.

TORTELLINI WITH SMOKED SALMON AND DILL WEED

Italian tortellini are traditionally made with meat, cheese, or vegetables, but these ones are filled with smoked salmon, ricotta, and dill weed and are served with a lemony sour cream sauce.

SERVES 4

Preparation time: 40 minutes plus 1 hour standing

Cooking time: 10 minutes

Attachments used

1 quantity basic pasta dough (page 38), rolled out
    to a setting 6 to 7 thickness

2 oz Parmesan cheese

5 oz smoked salmon

1$^1/_3$ cups ricotta cheese

2 Tbsp shredded lemon rind

2 Tbsp chopped fresh dill weed

Salt and freshly ground black pepper

1 egg, beaten

2 Tbsp butter

6 green onions, chopped

1$^1/_4$ cups sour or heavy cream

Fresh dill sprigs, to garnish

1 Using the Rotor Slicer/Shredder, with the fine shredding cone attached, grate the Parmesan cheese on speed 4.

2 Finely chop the smoked salmon. Place the ricotta cheese into the mixer bowl and, using the flat beater, beat the ricotta cheese on speed 4 until really creamy. Add 1 tablespoon of the lemon rind, 1 tablespoon of the dill weed, and seasoning to taste. Add the Parmesan cheese, chopped salmon, and then the beaten egg, and mix gently together.

3 Lay the sheets of rolled-out pasta onto a floured surface and cut into rectangular sheets, about 6 x 3 inches. Take one strip of pasta and cut out small rounds about 2 inches in diameter. Either place the stuffing in a piping bag fitted with a large potato nozzle or place teaspoonfuls in the center of the pasta rounds.

4 Moisten the edges of the pasta with a little water and fold over, encasing the filling. Holding a filled pasta, curve the pasta round to form a half-moon shape, and pinch the pointed edges together, to form a ring. Continue until all the pasta and stuffing have been used. Sprinkle with a little flour and leave to dry for about an hour.

5 Cook the tortellini in plenty of lightly salted boiling water for 3 to 4 minutes or until tender to the bite, *al dente*.

6 Meanwhile, heat the butter in a small pan, add the green onions, and fry gently for 2 minutes. Add the cream, the remaining lemon rind, and dill weed, and heat gently until hot, stirring occasionally.

7 Drain the cooked tortellini, then return to the pan. Pour over the sauce and serve garnished with the dill sprigs.

SPINACH AND PARMESAN GNOCCHI This spinach and Parmesan gnocchi, known as

Roman gnocchi, is made from semolina rather than potato. It is then cooked under the broiler or in the oven to make a hearty supper.

SERVES 4

Preparation time: 15 minutes

Cooking time: 20 minutes

Attachments used

2 oz Parmesan cheese

12 oz fresh spinach, washed thoroughly

2¹/₂ cups milk

³/₄ cup semolina

4 Tbsp softened butter

2 medium eggs, beaten

Salt and freshly ground black pepper

¹/₄ tsp freshly grated nutmeg

2 Tbsp butter, melted

Tomato passata (optional, page 37)

1 With the medium shredding cone on the Rotor Slicer/Shredder, on speed 4, grate the Parmesan. Place the spinach, with just the water clinging to the leaves, in a saucepan and cook for 3 to 4 minutes or until just wilted. Drain thoroughly and chop fine, then place in paper towels and squeeze out any excess moisture.

2 Pour the milk into a heavy-base pan and bring to a boil. Sprinkle in the semolina and stir until the mixture becomes really thick. Turn into the mixer bowl.

3 Add half the Parmesan, the spinach, and the softened butter. Using the flat beater, on speed 6, beat well, then gradually pour in the eggs and beat well. Add some seasoning with the nutmeg, then turn into a lightly oiled shallow dish. Leave until cold.

4 Cut the cold gnocchi into small rounds about 1 inch in size. Place in an oiled shallow gratin or baking dish and pour over the melted butter. Place under a preheated medium broiler and cook for 10 to 15 minutes or until heated through and golden brown. Sprinkle with the remaining Parmesan and serve with tomato passata.

FETTUCCINE ALLA ROMANA
A creamy pasta dish "in the Roman style," which in this case means a sauce made with hot pancetta, local white wine, and lots of cream and Parmesan.

SERVES 4

Preparation time: 20 minutes

Cooking time: 20 minutes

Attachments used

1 quantity basic pasta dough (page 38), rolled out to a setting 7 thickness

2 oz Parmesan cheese

4 tsp extra-virgin olive oil

2 tsp butter

1 clove garlic, minced

1/2 tsp paprika

5 oz pancetta or bacon, chopped

2/3 cup white wine

1/2 cup light cream

1 Attach the fettuccine tagliatelle cutter to the pasta maker and feed through the sheets of pasta dough on speed 2, cutting the strands to a spaghetti-length with scissors as they come through. Lay in a single layer on a clean dish towel or over a pasta drying rack if cooking immediately. If you want to use the pasta more than an hour after cutting it, toss it in a little flour to keep the fettuccine from sticking together and wrap the strands round to form nests. Leave on a dish towel to dry, then store in an airtight tin.

2 Using the Rotor Slicer/Shredder, with the fine shredding cone attached, on speed 4, shred the Parmesan cheese.

3 Meanwhile, heat the olive oil and butter in a saucepan and sauté the garlic, paprika, and bacon for 5 minutes or until softened. Add the wine and cream, bring to a boil, then reduce the heat and simmer for 10 minutes or until slightly reduced.

4 Cook the fettuccine in plenty of lightly salted boiling water for 1 to 2 minutes or until tender to the bite, *al dente*. Drain, stir into the sauce, and heat thoroughly. Serve immediately with the shredded Parmesan.

SPÄTZLE (German noodles) A cross between noodles and dumplings, these German spätzle are served with fried onions. If you prefer, you can scatter them with golden bread crumbs cooked in butter.

SERVES 4

Preparation time: 15 minutes plus 15 minutes standing time

Cooking time: 15 minutes

Attachments used

2 ³/₄ cups all-purpose flour
Pinch of freshly grated nutmeg
Salt and freshly ground black pepper
3 eggs
About ²/₃ cup cold water
1 large onion, cut into wedges
2 tsp oil
2 Tbsp unsalted butter

1 Sift the flour into the mixer bowl. Add the nutmeg and season generously with salt and pepper.

2 Beat the eggs in a jug with ¹/₂ cup of the water. With the flat beater on speed 1, gradually add the egg mixture to make a smooth, thick batter, adding the remaining water if needed. Cover the bowl and leave to stand for 15 minutes.

3 Meanwhile, using the Rotor Slicer/Shredder with the slicing cone attached, on speed 4, finely slice the onion. Melt the oil and butter in a large skillet and gently cook the onion for 10 to 15 minutes, or until very soft and just beginning to color.

4 Preheat the oven to its lowest setting. Bring a large pan of lightly salted water to a fast boil. Spread the dough thinly over a damp wooden chopping board.

5 Using a wet long knife, cut the dough into narrow strips and slide them off the corner of the board into the water. As soon as the noodles float to the surface, remove from the water with a slotted spoon, transfer to a heatproof dish, and keep warm in the oven.

6 When all the noodles are made, scatter with the fried onions, and serve straight away.

FISH, MEAT, AND POULTRY DISHES

CRAB CAKES WITH MANGO SAMBAL These spicy crab cakes are made with fresh

cilantro and lemon grass and are accompanied by a homemade Southeast Asian fruit sambal, or chutney.

SERVES 4

Preparation time: 15 minutes

Cooking time: 10 minutes

Attachments used

For the sambal

½ ripe mango

1 ripe avocado

1 green onion, chopped fine

1 small bird's eye chili or Thai chili, seeds removed and chopped fine

1 tsp Thai fish sauce

2 Tbsp lime juice

½ tsp sugar

1 Tbsp finely chopped fresh cilantro

½ Tbsp finely chopped fresh parsley

For the crab cakes

8 oz white crab meat, well drained

2 green onions, including green tops, chopped fine

2 Tbsp finely chopped fresh cilantro

2 tsp lime juice

1 tsp light soy sauce

1 tsp Thai fish sauce

1 red bird's eye chili or Thai chili, chopped fine

1 stalk lemon grass, chopped fine

1 tsp finely chopped fresh ginger

1 egg white

1 Tbsp cornstarch

Sunflower or vegetable oil, for shallow frying

Lime quarters, to serve

1   To prepare the sambal, chop the mango and avocado into ¼-inch dice, then add the remaining ingredients, and mix well. Set aside until needed.

2   Using the flat beater on speed 2, mix all the crab cake ingredients together except the egg white and cornstarch. Transfer to another bowl and set aside.

3   Clean the mixer bowl and dry thoroughly, then whisk the egg white and cornstarch together with the wire whip on speed 8 until white and fluffy but not firm. Fold the egg whites gently into the crab mixture using a metal spoon, ensuring that it is well blended.

4   Form the mixture into four large, round patties or into 16 small ones. Heat about ½ inch of oil in a heavy-base skillet and cook the crab cakes for about two minutes on each side, or one minute for the small cakes, until golden. Serve immediately with the mango and avocado sambal and lime quarters.

TERRINE OF FISH
All around the Mediterranean you find wonderful fish recipes like this simple Spanish fish terrine. It can be made with any white fish and is served in slices with a spoon of homemade mayonnaise.

SERVES 8

Preparation time: 10 minutes

Cooking time: 1 hour 25 minutes

Attachments used

1 lb white fish fillets, skinned

1 leek, roughly chopped

1 carrot, roughly chopped

8 eggs

Pinch of salt

Pinch of white pepper

1 cup heavy cream (whipping cream)

1 cup tomato passata (page 37)

$^1/_3$ cup fresh white bread crumbs

Sprigs of dill, to garnish

Mayonnaise, to serve (page 22)

1. Preheat the oven to 350°F. Put the fish in a large skillet and cover with water. Add the leek and carrot to the pan and cook over a medium heat for 10 minutes until the fish is cooked through. Remove the fish with a spatula and leave to cool. Discard the vegetables and cooking liquid.

2. Flake the fish, removing any bones. Put the eggs in the mixer bowl with the fish, salt and pepper, cream, and tomato sauce. With the flat beater, mix on speed 1 for 1 minute until well blended.

3. Lightly butter a 4-cup bread pan and coat the inside with the bread crumbs. Spoon the fish mixture into the pan and cover with foil. Put the loaf pan into a roasting pan half-filled with boiling water and cook in this bain-marie for 1 hour 15 minutes, or until set and cooked through. Unmold the loaf, slice, garnish with dill, and serve with mayonnaise.

FISH BALLS (Gedde Bollen) These tasty little Norwegian fish balls are made here with cod and are usually served with the creamy dill sauce poured over them, and a serving of boiled potatoes and simple buttered vegetables.

SERVES 4

Preparation time: 20 minutes plus 1 hour 30 minutes chilling time

Cooking time: 8 minutes

Attachments used

3 slices day-old white bread, crusts discarded

3 Tbsp heavy cream (whipping cream)

3 Tbsp milk

12 oz white fish fillet, such as cod, skinned and cut into strips

1 stick butter (¼ lb)

2 eggs

Pinch of freshly grated nutmeg

Salt and freshly ground black pepper

2¹/₂ cups fish stock

For the sauce

4 Tbsp heavy cream

2 Tbsp chopped fresh parsley or dill weed

1 Break the bread into small pieces and put in a saucepan. Drizzle over the cream and milk, then leave to soak for about 5 minutes.

2 Attach the food grinder, fitted with the fine grinding plate and, on speed 4, shred the fish into the mixer bowl.

3 Add about 1 tablespoon of the butter to the bread mixture in the saucepan, then stir over a low heat until it forms a smooth mixture that leaves the sides of the pan.

4 Add the bread to the shredded fish in the mixer bowl, with the eggs, nutmeg, and some salt and pepper. Mix together using the flat beater, on speed 2, until evenly blended.

5 Place the remaining butter in a saucepan and melt over a low heat. Using the flat beater, still on speed 2, slowly trickle the butter over the fish mixture in a steady stream until you have a smooth soft purée. Cover the mixer bowl and chill for at least one hour.

6 With dampened hands, shape the mixture into 20 small balls, each about the size of a walnut, and put them on a lightly floured plate. Chill them for a further 30 minutes, or freeze them briefly to make them very firm.

7 Bring the fish broth to a boil in a wide shallow saucepan or skillet, then reduce the heat so that it is gently simmering. Add the fish balls and poach for 7 to 8 minutes, turning them over halfway through. Using a slotted spoon, lift the fish balls into a serving dish and keep warm.

8 For the sauce, rapidly boil the broth until it reduces to about ¹/₂ cup. Stir in the cream and fresh herbs, and simmer for 2 minutes. Taste and season with a little salt and pepper, then drizzle over the fish balls.

LAKSA

LAKSA A spicy noodle soup from Southeast Asia, found all over Malaysia and Singapore, and made from chicken or seafood. Laksa is a meal in itself and is eaten with chopsticks and a spoon to scoop up all the tasty broth.

SERVES 4

Preparation time: 15 minutes

Cooking time: 25 minutes

Attachments used

1 large carrot

1 red bell pepper, deseeded

1 yellow bell pepper, deseeded

1–2 bird's eye chilies, deseeded

2 lemon grass stalks, outer leaves discarded

2 cloves garlic

1-inch piece gingerroot

2^1/$_2$ cups coconut milk

1^1/$_4$ cups chicken broth

Few saffron strands

Two 5-oz skinless, boneless chicken breasts, cut into thin strips

6 oz medium egg noodles

2 Tbsp cornstarch

Handful of chopped fresh cilantro leaves

1 cup peeled shrimp, thawed if frozen

1 Attach the slicing cone to the Rotor Slicer/Shredder and, on speed 4, slice the carrot and the red and yellow peppers.

2 Replace the slicing cone with the medium shredding cone and, on speed 4, chop the chilies, lemon grass, garlic, and ginger. Pour the coconut milk into a wok or saucepan with the broth and then add the chopped chili mixture. Simmer for 10 minutes.

3 Add the saffron strands with the carrot, pepper, and the chicken to the pan and bring to a boil, then simmer for a further 5 minutes.

4 Meanwhile, break the noodles into short lengths and cook in lightly boiling water for 5 minutes, drain, and keep warm.

5 Blend the cornstarch to a paste with 2 tablespoons of water, then stir into the wok or pan. Cook, stirring, until the mixture thickens. Stir in the chopped cilantro and the shrimp, cook for 2 minutes, or until the shrimp are thoroughly heated, then add the noodles, and serve.

SHRIMP AND GREEN ONION CRÊPES These Asian pancakes can be filled with chicken or

vegetables instead of shrimp. They can be prepared ahead, stored in the refrigerator, and heated through before adding the filling.

SERVES 4

Preparation time: 15 minutes plus 30

minutes standing time

Cooking time: 30 minutes

Attachments used

For the batter

3/4 cup all-purpose flour

Pinch of salt

1/2–1 tsp mild chili powder

1 medium egg, beaten

1 cup milk

2–3 Tbsp sunflower oil, for frying

For the filling

14-oz can chopped tomatoes

6 green onions, chopped

2 celery stalks, chopped fine

1 Tbsp sweet chili sauce, or to taste

2 Tbsp chopped fresh cilantro

1 Tbsp cornstarch

2 cups peeled shrimp, thawed if frozen

Salt and freshly ground black pepper

Fresh herbs, to garnish

1 Sift the flour, salt, and chili powder into the mixer bowl, make a well in the center, and pour in the beaten egg. Using the flat beater, on speed 2 to 4, gradually mix in the milk, stopping to scrape down the sides of the bowl as necessary. Continue to beat until a smooth batter is formed. Leave to stand for 30 minutes.

2 To make the filling, pour the tomatoes into a pan and add the green onions, celery, sweet chili sauce, and chopped cilantro. Simmer for 3 minutes, then blend the cornstarch with 2 tablespoons of water, and stir into the pan. Keep stirring until thickened. Mix in the peeled shrimp and add seasoning to taste. Keep warm.

3 Heat a small skillet and pour in a little of the oil. Swirl the skillet so that the base is completely coated with the hot oil, pouring off any

excess. Stir the batter, then pour 3 to 4 tablespoons into the pan and swirl to coat the base evenly. Cook for 2 minutes or until the bubbles on the top of the pancake burst, then turn the pancake over and cook the other side for 1 minute, or until done. Remove to a plate and stack between pieces of waxed paper. Keep warm while you make the rest of the panckaes.

4 Fill the cooked pancakes with the shrimp and green onion sauce, and serve garnished with fresh herbs.

POACHED SALMON
This spectacular British summer dish is a grand addition to any table and is ideal for a buffet party or to serve at a formal lunch. Accompany with homemade mayonnaise.

SERVES 10 TO 12

Preparation time: 30 minutes

Cooking time: 40 minutes

Attachments used

4 lb whole salmon, cleaned

1 onion, sliced

1 lemon, sliced

2 celery stalks, sliced

Few fresh parsley stalks

2 bay leaves

²/₃ cup medium-dry white wine

3³/₄ cups water

1 very large or 2 small cucumbers, peeled or unpeeled

Salad leaves and lemon wedges, to garnish

Homemade mayonnaise, to serve (page 22)

The Rotor Slicer/Shredder copes well with big quantities, but even if you are chopping, slicing, or shredding no more than just one or two vegetables, using this attachment rather than doing it by hand will save you time and effort. Here the slicing cone also produces beautifully even, wafer-thin slices of cucumber for decoration.

1 Lightly rinse the salmon and pat dry with paper towels. Leave the skin on the fish as this helps to keep the fish intact during cooking.

2 With the slicing cone on the Rotor Slicer/Shredder, on speed 4, slice the onion, lemon, and celery. Place, along with the parsley and bay leaves, in a fish pan or large saucepan. Add the wine with the water and bring to a boil. Reduce the heat and simmer for 10 minutes.

3 Place the fish on the fish pan trivet or in a tinfoil sling, lower into the simmering liquid, and bring to a boil. Calculate the cooking time by allowing 10 minutes per 1 lb, then simmer the fish for this amount of time. Remove from the heat and leave until cold in the cooking liquor.

4 When cold, remove the salmon from the fish pan and carefully peel off the skin using the back of a knife, discarding also the gills and eyes. Snip the backbone at the head and tail, then carefully ease the bone out. Place the fish on a serving platter.

5 With the slicing cone on the Rotor Slicer/Shredder, on speed 4, slice the cucumber and arrange over the salmon, to represent scales. Garnish around the base with salad leaves and lemon wedges, and serve with homemade mayonnaise.

CHICKEN, BELL PEPPER, AND MUSHROOM PARCELS

These little parcels are ideal for an informal lunch or supper party. Provided the chicken is fresh, the parcels can be made ahead of time and frozen.

SERVES 4

Preparation time: 25 minutes plus 30 minutes chilling time

Cooking time: 30 minutes

Attachments used

For the pastry

2 cups all-purpose flour

Pinch of salt

1¹/₄ sticks unsalted butter or margarine

1 small egg yolk

2 tsp cold water

Beaten egg, to glaze

For the filling

3 shallots

1 clove garlic

2–3 slices day-old bread, crusts discarded

2 oz button mushrooms

1 small red bell pepper, deseeded

1 Tbsp olive oil

Salt and freshly ground black pepper

Small handful fresh chervil or tarragon, chopped fine

Four 5-oz skinless, boneless chicken breasts

1 Lightly oil a cookie sheet. To make the pastry, sift the flour and salt into the mixer bowl. Cut the butter or margarine into cubes and add to the flour, together with the egg yolk and cold water. Using the flat beater, on speed 2, beat for about 1 minute or until the mixture forms a ball in the center of the bowl. Remove, knead lightly on a lightly floured surface, then wrap and chill in the refrigerator for 30 minutes.

2 Preheat the oven to 400°F. Attach the medium shredding cone to the Rotor Slicer/Shredder and, on speed 4, chop the shallots, garlic, bread, and mushrooms. Replace the medium shredding cone with the slicing cone and slice the red pepper. Heat the oil in a pan and sauté the shallot mixture for 2 minutes. Remove from the heat, and add seasoning to taste and the chopped herbs.

3 Roll the pastry out on a lightly floured surface and cut into four 8-inch squares. Divide the shallot mixture among the four pastry squares and place in the center of each pastry square. Rinse the chicken and pat dry, then place on top, and brush the edges of the pastry with a little beaten egg.

4 Fold the pastry over, completely encasing the chicken, and place seam-side down on the prepared cookie sheet. Use any trimmings to decorate the tops of the parcels. Brush with the beaten egg, then bake in the oven for 25 to 30 minutes.

TURKEY WITH GARBANZO PATTIES
This is a version of a Moroccan tagine, using turkey rather than chicken or lamb. A tagine is traditionally cooked in a conical-shaped dish called a tagine, but here it can be made in a saucepan.

SERVES 4

Preparation time: 15 minutes

Cooking time: 35 minutes

Attachments used

1 lb skinless, boneless turkey breast, diced

1 tsp turmeric

1 tsp paprika

2 Tbsp olive oil

1 onion, cut into wedges

2–3 cloves garlic, chopped

2^1/$_2$ cups chicken broth

3 oz dried apricots

1 cinnamon stick, broken in half

Salt and freshly ground black pepper

2 Tbsp cornstarch

2 Tbsp toasted almond slivers

1 Tbsp roughly chopped unsalted shelled pistachio nuts

1 Tbsp chopped fresh cilantro

For the garbanzo (chickpea) patties

14-oz can garbanzos (chickpeas), drained and rinsed

6 green onions

2 slices day-old bread, crusts discarded

1 small red chili, deseeded and chopped

Handful of fresh cilantro leaves, chopped

Salt and freshly ground black pepper

1 small egg yolk

About 2 Tbsp all-purpose flour

2 Tbsp olive oil

1 Coat the turkey in the turmeric and paprika. Heat the oil in a large pan and sauté the onion and garlic for 5 minutes. Add the turkey and continue to cook until the turkey is just brown.

2 Stir in the broth and bring to a boil, add the apricots, cinnamon, and seasoning, cover, and cook gently for 25 minutes, stirring occasionally during cooking. Blend the cornstarch with 2 tablespoons water to a smooth paste, stir into the turkey, and cook until slightly thickened.

3 Meanwhile, place the garbanzos (chickpeas) in the mixer bowl and, using the flat beater, on speed 2, beat them for a few minutes until broken down. Attach the medium shredding cone to the Rotor Slicer/ Shredder and, on speed 4 chop the green onions with the bread. Add to the garbanzos (chickpeas) together with the chili, cilantro, and seasoning.

4 Stir the egg yolk into the mixture and mix well. Scrape out of the bowl and shape into small rounds. Coat in the flour.

5 Heat the oil in a skillet and fry the patties on both sides for about 4 minutes, or until golden and heated through.

6 Sprinkle the turkey with the almonds, pistachio nuts, and chopped cilantro, and serve with the garbanzo (chickpea) patties and couscous or rice.

CHICKEN TANDOORI
This Indian dish is traditionally baked in a very hot clay tandoor oven, heated with charcoal. Barbecuing your chicken tandoori will create a similar smoky flavor and the marinade can be used to coat any meat or seafood.

SERVES 4

Preparation time: 40 minutes plus marinating time

Cooking time: 25 minutes

Attachments used

1¹/₂ Tbsp coriander seeds
1¹/₂ Tbsp cumin seeds
1 hot red chili, such as bird's eye, deseeded
2 large cloves garlic
2-inch piece gingerroot
2 Tbsp lemon juice
1 tsp garam masala
²/₃ cup low-fat plain yogurt
Few drops of red food coloring
Salt and freshly ground black pepper
Four 5-oz skinless, boneless chicken breasts
Lime wedges and fresh herbs, to garnish

1 Dry-fry the coriander and cumin seeds for 3 to 4 minutes, stirring frequently and taking care not to burn the spices. Remove, cool, then grind in a pestle and mortar.

2 Attach the medium shredding cone to the Rotor Slicer/Shredder and, on speed 4, grind the chili, garlic, and ginger into the mixer bowl. Stir in the ground spices, then the lemon juice, and mix to a paste. Add the garam masala, the yogurt, and a few drops of food coloring to give a good red color, then season.

3 Rinse the chicken and pat dry. Make three slashes across each breast and place in a shallow dish. Pour over the tandoori paste, cover, and leave to marinate for at least 6 hours, spooning the marinade over the chicken occasionally, or, if time permits, leave overnight.

4 When ready to cook, preheat the broiler and line the broiler rack with tinfoil, or light the barbecue 20 minutes before cooking. Drain the chicken and cook for 20 to 25 minutes or until cooked and the juices run clear. Turn the chicken frequently during cooking and brush occasionally with the marinade. Serve garnished with lime wedges and fresh herbs.

CHICKEN WITH BELL PEPPERS
This tasty Southeast Asian stir-fry uses fresh kaffir lime leaves. If you have difficulty finding fresh ones, most supermarkets sell dried ones, or you could just leave them out.

SERVES 4

Preparation time: 10 minutes

Cooking time: 12 minutes

Attachments used

8 oz cellophane noodles

2-inch piece gingerroot

2 lemon grass stalks, outer leaves discarded

2–4 cloves garlic

1 red bell pepper, deseeded

1 yellow bell pepper, deseeded

1 green bell pepper. deseeded

2 carrots

Two 5-oz skinless, boneless chicken breasts

2 Tbsp peanut oil

1–2 bird's eye chilies, deseeded and chopped

2 kaffir lime leaves

2 Tbsp light soy sauce

1 Tbsp Thai fish sauce

2 Tbsp chopped fresh cilantro

1 Soak the cellophane noodles in boiling water for 4 minutes, then drain and set aside until required.

2 With the medium shredding cone on the Rotor Slicer/Shredder, on speed 4, shred the ginger, lemon grass, and garlic. Change to the slicing cone and, still on speed 4, slice the peppers and then the carrots.

3 Cut the chicken into strips. Heat a wok until hot then add the oil, heat for 30 seconds, and stir-fry the chili, lime leaves, ginger, lemon grass, and garlic for 1 minute. Add the chicken strips and continue to stir-fry for 3 minutes, or until brown.

4 Add the pepper and carrot and stir-fry for 4 minutes. Add the noodles and stir-fry for 2 minutes. Pour in the soy sauce and Thai fish sauce, and stir-fry for another 2 minutes, or until the chicken is completely cooked through. Sprinkle with the chopped cilantro and serve immediately.

LAMB EN CROÛTE
This lamb version of bœuf en croûte uses flaky pastry, but you could also use shortcrust pastry or a brioche dough to enclose the lamb and herb filling.

SERVES 8

Preparation time: 30 minutes

Cooking time: 20 minutes

Attachments used

1 stick butter (¼ lb)

Eight 4-oz lamb fillets, approx. 4 inches long

Salt and freshly ground black pepper

2 Tbsp chopped fresh chervil

3 Tbsp chopped fresh tarragon

6 fresh basil leaves, chopped

1 Tbsp extra-virgin olive oil

1 quantity flaky pastry, rolled out to 8 sheets 6 x 6 inches each (page 118)

1 egg yolk

1 cup lamb or beef broth

2 Tbsp cognac

1 Preheat the oven to 400°F. Melt half of the butter in a large skillet and rub the lamb with the salt and pepper. Sear both sides of the meat for 30 seconds on high heat. Remove from the pan immediately and drain on a wire rack or inverted plate so that the meat is not lying in its own juices. Reserve the lamb juices. Leave to cool and set aside.

2 In a bowl, mix together the herbs and olive oil, and season with salt and pepper. The herb mixture should be a thick paste and should not be runny at all.

3 Lay out the sheets of flaky pastry. Spread 1 teaspoon of the herb mixture onto each.

4 Pat dry the lamb with paper towels and place one piece of meat onto each sheet of pastry. Top the meat with 1 more teaspoon of the herb mixture and fold the pastry into little parcels. Brush the ends with some cold water and seal the parcels. Turn them over and make small slits on top with a sharp knife.

5 Whisk the egg yolk with some water and brush over the lamb parcels. Place in the oven for 12 to 14 minutes until golden brown. Add the remaining butter and the cognac to the lamb juices in a small saucepan and season with salt and pepper. Heat until slightly reduced to a gravy consistency.

6 Serve the lamb parcels with the gravy and accompany with spring vegetables and parsley-buttered potatoes.

PORK WITH CALVADOS AND APPLES This version of the classic Normandy and Brittany

dish, Poulet Vallée d'Auge, is made from apples, crème fraîche, and Calvados, all specialties of Northwest France.

SERVES 4

Preparation time: 15 minutes

Cooking time: 1 hour 15 minutes

Attachments used

1 onion

2–3 cloves garlic

2 tart apples (such as Granny Smith), peeled and cored

3 Tbsp unsalted butter

1 lb pork fillet, cut into $^1/_2$-inch slices

2 Tbsp all-purpose flour

3 Tbsp Calvados or other apple liqueur

1$^3/_4$ cups chicken broth

Salt and freshly ground black pepper

1 tsp granulated brown sugar

2 Tbsp chopped fresh sage

4 Tbsp crème fraîche

Apple slices, to garnish

1 Preheat the oven to 350°F. Attach the slicing cone to the Rotor Slicer/Shredder and, on speed 4, slice the onion and garlic, then the apples separately. Melt half of the butter in a skillet and sauté the onion and garlic for 3 minutes, add the apples, and continue to sauté for a further 2 minutes. Remove with a draining spoon and reserve.

2 Heat the remaining butter in the pan, add the pork, and sauté for 5 minutes, then sprinkle in the flour and cook for 2 minutes. Add the Calvados, heat for 1 minute, then take the pan off the heat, and set alight with a match, taking care that you stand well back, and keeping a pan lid handy for emergencies. When the flames have subsided, stir in the broth, add the onion mixture, and return to the heat. Cook, stirring, until the mixture thickens. Add some salt and pepper, the sugar, and 1 tablespoon of the sage, and pour into a casserole.

3 Cook in the oven for 1 hour or until the pork is tender. Stir in the crème fraîche, sprinkle with the remaining sage, and garnish with apple slices.

VEAL IN TUNA SAUCE (Vitello Tonnato) A northern Italian dish that needs to be made the day before and chilled

overnight in the refrigerator. If you're using a leg of veal, ask your butcher to bone it, and tie it in a neat roll.

SERVES 6

Preparation time: 25 minutes plus 24 hours
marinating and 3 hours chilling

Cooking time: 1 hour

Attachments used

1 onion, cut into wedges

1 carrot

1 stalk celery

1$\frac{1}{2}$-lb piece of leg or loin of veal

1 bay leaf

2 whole cloves

4$\frac{1}{2}$ cups dry white wine, preferably Italian

1 tsp salt

7 oz canned tuna, drained

4 anchovy fillets, rinsed

2 Tbsp capers in vinegar

1 lemon

2 egg yolks

1 Tbsp white wine vinegar

Freshly ground black pepper

$\frac{2}{3}$ cup olive oil

1 Using the Rotor Slicer/Shredder, fitted with the slicing cone, on speed 4, slice the onion, carrot, and celery into a large glass or stainless steel bowl. Make a hollow in the vegetables and put the meat in it. Add the bay leaf and cloves and pour over the wine. Cover and leave in the refrigerator for 24 hours, turning the meat several times.

2 Next day, put the meat into a saucepan with the vegetables, marinade, and the bones if you have them. Sprinkle over the salt and add just enough water to barely cover. Bring to a boil, reduce the heat, cover, and simmer for 45 minutes to 1 hour, or until the meat is cooked through and tender. Remove from the heat and allow to cool in the pan.

3 Using the food grinder, with the fine grinding plate attached, on speed 4, mince the tuna, anchovy fillets, and 1 tablespoon of the capers into the mixer bowl. Squeeze in the juice of half the lemon, then add the egg yolks, vinegar, and black pepper. Change to the wire whip and beat the mixture on speed 4 for a few seconds.

4 On speed 6, add the oil a little at a time in a thin stream, whisking well between each addition, until the sauce is thick and shiny. Whisk in about 2 tablespoons of the veal broth from the pan to give the sauce the consistency of thin cream. Taste and adjust the seasoning if necessary.

5 Slice the veal as thinly as possible and arrange on a serving dish. Spoon over the tuna sauce, cover, and refrigerate for at least 3 hours. Serve garnished with the remaining capers and remaining lemon half, sliced thin.

MEAT CAKES (Kjottkaker) One of Norway's most popular dishes, these ground beef patties are made in every home to a family recipe, fried until crispy, and often served with a sauce.

SERVES 4

Preparation time: 20 minutes

Cooking time: 40 minutes

Attachments used

4 slices white bread, crusts discarded

2 Tbsp milk

1 lb lean beef (sirloin, round, or chuck steak)

1 onion, cut into wedges

1 egg

Salt and freshly ground black pepper

2 Tbsp all-purpose flour

2 Tbsp sunflower oil

1 Preheat the oven to 250ºF. Put the bread on a cookie sheet and bake for 20 minutes, turning occasionally until dry.

2 Using the Rotor Slicer/Shredder with the medium shredding cone attached, on speed 4, shred the bread into the bowl. Sprinkle over the milk and leave to soak for 5 minutes.

3 Using the food grinder, fitted with the coarse grinding plate, on speed 4, shred the beef into the bowl, followed by the onion. Add the egg and season well with salt and pepper. Mix together using the flat beater, on speed 4, until evenly blended.

4 Divide the mixture into four equal portions and shape each into an oval about 4 inches long and 2 inches wide. Lightly dust them with flour and chill if time allows.

5 Heat the oil in a skillet and fry the meat cakes for 7 to 8 minutes on each side, or until nicely brown and cooked through. Drain on paper towels and serve hot.

Raw meat and fish is easier to feed through the food grinder if it is cut into strips, rather than chunks. If you want your meat extra tender, you can put it through the food grinder twice, first through the coarse plate, then through the fine, although do not mince the meat twice if it is quite fatty.

FILET AMÉRICAIN WITH ORIGINAL BELGIAN FRITES The Filet

Américain is the perfect companion to the very finest frites in the world. In Belgium it is often served on a slice of toast, and is known as "toast cannibal."

SERVES 6

Preparation time: 15 minutes, plus chilling time

Cooking time: 1 hour

Attachments used

1³/₄ lb lean beef steak such as fillet or round

12 gherkins, drained thoroughly

¹/₂ small onion, peeled

4 fresh, organic, medium egg yolks

2 Tbsp olive oil

2 Tbsp capers, drained thoroughly

1 Tbsp freshly chopped parsley

1 Tbsp Worcestershire sauce

Salt and freshly ground black pepper

For the frites

2 lb floury potatoes, such as Yukon Gold, peeled

Oil for deep frying

1 Trim the steak, discarding any fat or gristle, and cut into strips or small cubes. Attach the food grinder fitted with the fine grinding plate and place the mixer bowl underneath. Grind the beef on speed 4 into the bowl. Do this twice so that the meat is finely ground.

2 Clean the fine plate and the food grinder and then pass the gherkins and onion through and into the mixer bowl. Add all the remaining ingredients with seasoning to taste, and mix well using the flat beater.

3 Divide into 4 and shape into steaks. Cover lightly and keep in the refrigerator until required.

4 Cut the potatoes into ¹/₂-inch slices and then into thin strips. Cover completely with cold water and leave for 30 minutes to remove any excess starch. Drain thoroughly and pat dry.

5 Heat the oil in a deep fryer to 375°F. Place a layer of potatoes in the frying basket and lower carefully into the hot oil. Cook for 5 minutes or until the potato frites are soft but still white. Remove and drain thoroughly. Repeat with the remaining frites.

6 Just before serving, reheat the oil to 375°F, then place a layer of the blanched frites in the frying basket. Plunge into hot oil and cook for 3 to 5 minutes or until golden brown and crisp. Remove and drain on paper towels, and serve with the Filet Américain.

QUICHE LORRAINE A specialty of the Alsace-Lorraine region of France, this quiche is made from a crisp, shortcrust pastry filled with an egg, cream, cheese, and bacon mixture.

SERVES 4

Preparation time: 25 minutes plus 30 minutes chilling time

Cooking time: 50 minutes

1²/₃ cups all-purpose flour

Pinch of salt

1 stick butter (¼ lb)

Cold water

1 small onion, chopped fine

4 slices good-quality bacon, chopped fine

3 eggs, beaten

1³/₄ cups milk, or milk and light cream mixed

3 oz Gruyère cheese, grated fine

Salt and freshly ground black pepper to taste

Attachments used

1 Place a cookie sheet in the oven and preheat the oven to 425°F.

2 To make the pastry, sift the flour and salt into the mixer bowl. Cut the butter into cubes. Using the flat beater, on speed 2, beat until well blended. Add just enough iced water to make a smooth dough, then remove, and knead lightly on a lightly floured surface. Shape the dough into a ball, wrap in plastic wrap, and chill in the refrigerator for 30 minutes.

3 Roll the pastry out into a circle on a lightly floured surface and use to line an 8-inch greased tart pan, about 2 inches deep.

4 Cook the chopped onion and bacon together for five minutes over a gentle heat in a nonstick skillet. Spoon into the tart pan.

5 Using the flat beater on speed 4, beat the eggs into the milk, or milk and cream, then add most of the cheese with some salt and pepper, and beat again. Pour the mixture over the bacon and onion, and scatter the remaining cheese on top.

6 Place the quiche on the hot cookie sheet and bake for 10 minutes. Lower the temperature to 375°F and continue baking for another 30 to 35 minutes, until the filling is just set. Allow to cool slightly before cutting. Serve the quiche warm or cold.

MEATBALLS (Polpette) These little beef meatballs are served in Italy traditionally with grilled eggplant or just some bread, as a main course, following a pasta appetizer. You could use pork instead of beef and basil instead of parsley.

SERVES 4

Preparation time: 20 minutes

Cooking time: 30 minutes

Attachments used

1–2 slices day-old white bread, crusts discarded

2 oz Parmesan cheese

1 carrot

12 oz lean beef (round or chuck steak)

1 onion, quartered

1 clove garlic

1 stalk celery

Handful fresh parsley leaves, chopped fine

1 egg

1 Tbsp olive oil

1 Preheat the oven to 275ºF. Bake the slices of bread on a cookie sheet for about 20 minutes, turning several times, until dried out. Leave to cool.

2 Turn up the oven to 350ºF. Using the Rotor Slicer/Shredder, with the fine shredding cone attached, on speed 4, shred the Parmesan into the mixer bowl. Remove 2 tablespoons of the shredded cheese and set aside. Shred the bread, then the carrot, into the bowl.

3 Attach the food grinder, fitted with the fine grinding plate, and, on speed 4, grind the beef into the mixer bowl, followed by the onion, garlic, and celery.

4 Change to the flat beater, add the parsley, egg, and olive oil to the bowl and, on speed 4, mix together until evenly blended. With dampened hands, shape the mixture into 20 small balls and place on a lightly oiled cookie sheet. Bake for about 30 minutes, or until piping hot and cooked through.

5 Sprinkle with the reserved Parmesan and serve immediately with broiled vegetables and perhaps some bread.

SWEDISH MEATBALLS
These spicy meatballs are made from beef and mashed potato, and come with a little gravy made from the meat juices and cream. Serve them with noodles or potatoes.

SERVES 4

Preparation time: 20 minutes plus 1 hour chilling time

Cooking time: 15 minutes

Attachments used

1 onion, cut into wedges

1 medium potato, cut into wedges

1 lb lean beef (sirloin or blade), trimmed and cut into strips

2 Tbsp butter

3 Tbsp fine dried bread crumbs

1/4 tsp dried crushed chili

1 1/4 cups heavy cream (whipping cream)

Salt and freshly ground black pepper

1 medium egg

1 Tbsp chopped fresh parsley

3 Tbsp oil

1 Tbsp flour

1 Using the Rotor Slicer/Shredder with the medium shredding cone attached, on speed 4, shred the onion into the mixer bowl. Remove the bowl, place a saucepan underneath the mixer and, still on speed 4, shred the potato into the pan. Cover with cold water and cook for 12 minutes or until tender. Drain the potato thoroughly, mash, and reserve.

2 Attach the food grinder, fitted with the fine grinding plate and, on speed 4, shred the beef into the bowl. Do this twice so that the meat is ground fine.

3 Heat 1 tablespoon of the butter in a small saucepan and sauté the onion for 5 minutes, stirring frequently until softened, then pour into the mixer bowl. Add the bread crumbs with the chili, about 3 tablespoons of the heavy cream, the mashed potato, seasoning, egg, and parsley. With the flat beater, beat the mixture on speed 6 until smooth and fluffy.

4 Shape into about 32 small meatballs and place on one or two trays. Cover with plastic wrap and chill in the refrigerator for 1 hour.

In this recipe, the Rotor Slicer/Shredder has prepared the onion and potato, and the grinder has ground the meat; it is then that the flat beater is used for blending the ingredients together. Unlike a food processor blade, it doesn't just keep chopping everything down.

5 When ready to cook, heat the remaining butter and oil in a skillet. Cook the meatballs in the pan for 8 to 10 minutes or until thoroughly cooked, remove from the pan, and drain well on paper towels.

6 Pour off the excess butter and oil from the pan, sprinkle in the flour, and cook, scraping up the sediment that is left in the bottom. Pour in the remaining cream and cook, stirring, until the sauce comes to a boil. Return the meatballs to the pan and heat through gently until piping hot.

SPICY SAUSAGES These pork sausages are used in lots of hearty winter stews, mixed with beans, lentils, and

tomatoes. You could roll the sausages by hand, but the sausage stuffer makes light work of producing the links.

SERVES 6

Preparation time: 30 minutes

Cooking time: 10 minutes

Attachments used

2 lb pork belly (ask your butcher), rind and bones removed, cut into
    1-inch cubes

2 Tbsp paprika

2 tsp dried hot pepper flakes

2 Tbsp fennel seeds

Salt and freshly ground black pepper

Natural or synthetic casings (optional)

All-purpose flour, for dusting (optional)

Oil, for frying

Tomato passata (page 37), to serve

1   Chill the meat before putting through the food grinder, on speed 4, first through the coarse plate and then through the fine plate.

2   In the mixer bowl, and using the flat beater on speed 2 to 4, mix the spices and seasoning into the ground pork.

3   If using the sausage stuffer, soak the natural casings in cold water for 30 minutes, then rinse thoroughly. Grease the sausage stuffer tube and slide the casing on tightly, tying off the end. On speed 4, feed through the pork mixture, twisting and shaping the sausages into small links. Roll the sausages in a little all-purpose flour before cooking.

4   Heat a little oil in a skillet and fry the sausages, turning two or three times, until brown. Serve hot, with tomato passata.

BRATWURST A very popular pale German sausage made from a mixture of ground pork and veal. The sausages are fried or broiled

and are often served with crisp fried potatoes and sauerkraut.

SERVES 3 TO 4

Preparation time: 15 minutes

Cooking time: 20 minutes

Attachments used

10 oz lean pork fillet, trimmed

5 oz veal escalope or lean beef (such as round steak)

3 small shallots, peeled and cut into wedges

1/3 cup fresh white bread crumbs

1 tsp ground ginger

1 tsp ground coriander

1/2 tsp caraway seeds

1/4–1/2 tsp freshly grated nutmeg

Salt and freshly ground black pepper

6–8 natural or synthetic casings

Oil, for frying

1   Chill the meat and cut into strips before putting through the food grinder with the shallots, on speed 4, first through the coarse plate and then through the fine plate.

2   In the mixer bowl, and using the flat beater on speed 2 to 4, mix the bread crumbs, spices, and seasoning into the ground meat.

3   Before using the sausage stuffer, soak the natural casings in cold water for 30 minutes, then rinse thoroughly. Grease the sausage stuffer tube and slide the casing on tightly, tying off the end. On speed 4, feed through the meat mixture, twisting the sausages into small links

4   Heat a little oil in a skillet and fry the sausages for 15 to 20 minutes, turning two or three times, until brown.

BABY CHICKEN WITH CARROTS
This recipe for baby food is a perfect introduction to grown-up tastes. It is suitable for babies over six months old and if you are making extra, freeze what you do not need immediately in ice cube trays, remembering to label and date it clearly.

MAKES ENOUGH FOR 4 BABY MEALS

Preparation time: 10 minutes

Cooking time: 25 minutes

1 Tbsp butter

1/2 skinless, boneless chicken breast, diced

1 carrot, chopped

1 medium potato, chopped

A few broccoli florets

2 tomatoes, skinned and deseeded

1 1/4 cups chicken broth

Blender used

1 Heat the butter in a skillet and sauté the chicken for 5 minutes or until brown. Add the vegetables with the tomatoes and broth, and bring to a boil. Reduce the heat, cover, and cook over a gentle heat for 12 minutes or until the chicken and vegetables are completely cooked through.

2 Remove from the heat, cool slightly, then mix in the blender on purée speed until the mixture reaches the right consistency. Serve immediately, and freeze any extra in ice cube trays.

BABY PEACH FOOL
This baby pudding is suitable for babies over six months of age. You can use almost any fresh or cooked fruit for the recipe, but try to choose fruit that is very ripe and naturally sweet.

MAKES ENOUGH FOR 2 BABY MEALS

Preparation time: 5 minutes

1 ripe peach

3 Tbsp plain fromage blanc (fresh cream cheese)

1 Tbsp baby rice

1 Tbsp sugar (optional)

Baby rusk or sponge finger cookie (optional)

Blender used

1 Plunge the peach into hot water and leave it for a few minutes. Pour away the water, carefully peel the peach, and cut it in half. Discard the pit.

2 Place the peach in the blender with the fromage blanc and the baby rice, and blend on purée speed until smooth.

3 Taste and, if necessary, add a little sugar. Serve with a baby rusk or sponge finger cookie.

VEGETABLE DISHES

MASHED POTATOES
You can serve this mash topped with sour cream and scattered with chopped green onions or chives, or lay slices of smoked salmon or baked or pan-fried cod on top for a quick meal.

SERVES 6 TO 8

Preparation time: 15 minutes

Cooking time: 20 minutes

Attachments used

2 lb potatoes, cut into quarters
1 stick butter (¼ lb), cut into small cubes
$^1/_2$–$^2/_3$ cup heavy cream or whole milk
Salt and freshly ground black pepper

1 Boil the potatoes in salted water until tender, then drain them well. Place the cooked potatoes in the mixer bowl and, using the flat beater on speed 2 to 4, mash them well, then add the butter.

2 Heat the cream or milk, not allowing it to boil, and add it to the potatoes. Beat again until fluffy. Season as required with salt and black pepper, and serve immediately.

COLCANNON
An Irish potato dish traditionally eaten at Hallowe'en, colcannon is often served in individual pots with a pool of melted butter in the middle of the potato for dipping each forkful of mash into.

SERVES 8

Preparation time: 10 minutes

Cooking time: 20 minutes

Attachments used

3 lb potatoes
1$^1/_2$ sticks butter (6 oz)
2 Tbsp milk
6 green onions or 3 Tbsp chives, chopped
1 lb cooked kale or green cabbage, chopped fine
Salt and freshly ground black pepper
Grated nutmeg

1 Cut the potatoes into quarters and cook in boiling water for 20 minutes until softened and cooked through. Drain well and transfer to the mixer bowl. Add the butter and milk.

2 Using the flat beater, beat together for 30 seconds on speed 2. Reduce to speed 1 and add the green onions or chives and the kale or cabbage. Season well.

3 Spoon the colcannon into a warm serving dish, grate a little nutmeg over the top, and serve.

HERB SAUCE WITH NEW POTATOES
There is no single recipe for this well-loved German sauce, but all use the same spring herbs. Serve over new potatoes or with boiled beef, salted brisket, or steamed fish.

SERVES 6

Preparation time: 15 minutes plus 30 minutes infusing and 30 minutes chilling time

Cooking time: 20 minutes

Attachments used

6 tsp of various fresh green herbs, such as sorrel, chervil, parsley, or
   watercress
2 medium shallots
3 Tbsp white wine vinegar
4 medium eggs, hard-cooked and shelled
1¹/₄ cups heavy or light cream
Salt and freshly ground black pepper
1 Tbsp mustard
4 Tbsp olive oil
1¹/₂ lb new potatoes

1 Finely chop all the herbs and watercress. Using the Rotor Slicer/Shredder fitted with the medium shredding cone, on speed 4, finely chop the shallots. Add to the herbs and pour over the vinegar, then cover, and leave to stand for 30 minutes.

2 Pass the eggs through the Rotor Slicer/Shredder, still fitted with the medium shredding cone, on speed 4, into the mixer bowl. Attach the flat beater and, on speed 4, gradually pour the cream into the chopped eggs. Add salt and pepper to taste with the mustard, then gradually stir in the oil. Add the chopped herbs with the vinegar and scrape into a serving bowl. Cover and leave in the refrigerator for 30 minutes.

3 Meanwhile, cook the potatoes in lightly salted boiling water until tender. Drain, then stir the green sauce, and pour over the hot potatoes.

PISSALADIÈRE
A specialty of Nice, this French version of pizza can be made with either a bread dough, as here, or a pastry base, and can be served hot or cold as just a snack or lunch.

SERVES 6

Preparation time: 20 minutes plus 1 hour rising time

Cooking time: 45 minutes

Attachments used

4 cups all-purpose flour

1 heaping tsp active dry yeast

$1/2$ tsp salt

1 cup warm water

$1^1/4$ lb onions

4 Tbsp olive oil

2 tsp herbes de Provence

30 anchovy fillets in oil

20 black olives, pitted and halved

1 Put the flour, yeast, and salt in the mixer bowl. With the dough hook, on speed 2, gradually add the warm water until a soft dough forms. Roll the dough out on a lightly floured surface to a round, $1/2$ inch in thickness.

2 Fold the edge of the round back on itself to form a raised edge. Transfer the dough to a cookie sheet covered in waxed paper and leave in a warm, draft-free place to rise for 1 hour.

3 Meanwhile, using the Rotor Slicer/Shredder, with the slicing cone attached, on speed 4, slice the onions. Heat the olive oil in a saucepan and cook the onions with 1 teaspoon of the herbes de Provence over a medium heat until the onions are translucent. Transfer to a plate and leave to cool.

4 Preheat the oven to 400ºF. Once the dough has risen, sprinkle the onion mixture and the remaining herbs over the surface. Arrange the anchovies on top, crossing them to make a diamond pattern. Place a piece of olive inside each diamond. Cook for 10 minutes then reduce the oven temperature to 375ºF. Cook for a further 20 to 25 minutes until cooked through.

TORTA PASQUALINA (Savory Easter tart) This unusual specialty from Genoa used to be made mainly at Easter and takes

a bit of effort. To make it easier, you could replace the homemade pastry with frozen puff pastry.

SERVES 10

Preparation time: 1 hour plus 1 hour resting time

Cooking time: 1 hour 20 minutes

Attachments used

For the pastry

4 cups all-purpose flour

Pinch of salt

2 Tbsp olive oil

1¼ cups water

For the filling

2 lb fresh spinach, tough stems removed

Salt and freshly ground black pepper

1–2 Tbsp chopped fresh marjoram

1 large dry bread roll, crusts removed

About ½ cup milk

3 oz Parmesan cheese

8 medium eggs

2 cups ricotta cheese

5–6 Tbsp olive oil

4 Tbsp butter

1 Preheat the oven to 400°F and brush a 10-inch springform pan with a little oil. Sift the flour with the salt into the mixer bowl. Using the dough hook, on speed 1, pour in the olive oil, then slowly pour in sufficient water to form a smooth but not sticky dough. Continue to knead the mixture with the dough hook on speed 2 for about 5 minutes until really smooth and pliable. Divide into 12 pieces, shape into balls, and place on a lightly floured dish towel. Cover with a damp dish towel and leave to rest for 1 hour.

2 Meanwhile, prepare the filling. Place the spinach in a large saucepan and cook until just wilted with only the water left clinging to the leaves, adding a little salt. Drain thoroughly, squeezing out any excess liquid, then chop fine, season with salt and pepper to taste, and add the marjoram.

3 Cut the bread roll into small pieces and soak in the milk. Attach the Rotor Slicer/Shredder fitted with the fine shredding cone, and shred the Parmesan cheese into the mixer bowl, on speed 4. Place in a separate bowl.

4 Break two of the eggs into the mixer bowl and, with the flat beater on speed 4, beat the eggs until blended, then beat in 2 tablespoons of the Parmesan cheese. Squeeze out any excess moisture from the bread roll and beat into the egg mixture. Add the ricotta cheese and beat on speed 2 until well blended, then beat in the chopped spinach.

5 Roll out one of the balls of pastry on a lightly floured surface, carefully stretching the pastry by hand in all directions like strudel pastry to make it as thin as possible. Arrange the pastry in the base of the oiled pan so that the pastry overhangs the edge by about ½ inch. Lightly brush with oil. Continue this for five further balls of pastry, brushing each layer with oil.

6 Spread the prepared filling on top of the six layers of pastry, smooth the top, and brush with a little more oil. Using the back of a spoon, make six evenly spaced indentations in the filling and place a small pat of butter in each. Break an egg into each of the indentations, taking care not to break the yolks. Season with salt and pepper and sprinkle with the remaining Parmesan cheese.

7 Roll out the remaining balls of pastry and arrange on top, brushing each layer with oil as for the base. Place the remaining butter in small pieces round the edge of the pastry. Roll the overhanging pastry inwards over the butter and press down.

8 Brush the top with a little oil and carefully pierce in two to three places so that the steam can escape, then bake in the oven for 1 hour 15 minutes or until golden brown. Serve warm or cold.

LITTLE STUFFED VEGETABLES (Petits Légumes Farcis) This Provençal dish makes use of whatever is

in season – try stuffing small red, yellow, or green bell peppers or zucchini. It can be eaten hot or cold for a simple summer lunch.

SERVES 4

Preparation time: 25 minutes

Cooking time: 40 minutes

Attachments used

4 large onions

4 large tomatoes

4 oz bacon, diced

9 oz cooked pork

1 Tbsp chopped fresh parsley

Salt and freshly ground black pepper

3 Tbsp sour cream

1 egg yolk

2 Tbsp olive oil

1 Preheat the oven to 350ºF. Peel the onions, cut off a lid from each one, and place them all in salted boiling water for 10 minutes. Drain and scoop out the insides, and chop fine, using the Rotor Slicer/Shredder fitted with the fine shredding cone.

2 Cut lids off the tomatoes and scoop out the insides. Dust the insides of the tomatoes with salt and place upside down on paper towels.

3 Fry the bacon for 3 minutes. Add the chopped onion and sauté for 3 minutes.

4 Dice the cooked pork and mix with the parsley, bacon, and onion, and some seasoning. Pass the mixture through the food grinder fitted with the coarse grinding plate, on speed 4, then add the sour cream and egg yolk and, using the flat beater, mix in well.

5 Spoon the filling into the vegetables and replace the lids. Place in a roasting pan with a little water in the bottom and drizzle with the olive oil. Cook in the oven for 35 minutes, basting occasionally.

VICHY CARROTS
(Carottes Vichy) A dish of slow-cooked glazed carrots, which were originally cooked in Vichy mineral water from the Bourbonnais area of France, also famous for its root vegetables.

SERVES 4

Preparation time: 5 minutes

Cooking time: 1 hour

Attachments used

1 lb carrots

1 large onion

2–4 cloves garlic

1 bouquet garni (thyme, rosemary, and parsley)

1 Tbsp butter

1 tsp superfine sugar

Salt and freshly ground black pepper

1/2 cup water

1 Tbsp chopped fresh parsley

1 Preheat the oven to 350ºF. Using the Rotor Slicer/Shredder, with the slicing cone attached, on speed 4, slice the carrots, onion, and garlic, and place in an ovenproof dish.

2 Add the remaining ingredients, except for the parsley, cover, and cook in the oven for 1 hour or until the carrots are tender. Sprinkle with the chopped parsley and serve immediately.

The Rotor Slicer/Shredder can slice, shred, or mince straight into the mixer bowl, an oven dish or saucepan. To speed things up, do all your chopping before you start – you can even switch from one cone to another without removing the attachment from the KitchenAid mixer.

BRAISED RED CABBAGE
In this German cabbage dish, extra sweetness comes from the apple and apple juice.

If you want a less sweet dish, replace the juice with more red wine or water.

SERVES 4 TO 6

Preparation time: 10 minutes

Cooking time: 1 hour 30 minutes

Attachments used

1 onion

1 large tart apple (such as Granny Smith), peeled and cored

1/2 cup balsamic vinegar

2 Tbsp superfine sugar

3/4 stick butter (3 oz)

1/2 cup red wine

1/2 cup apple juice

4 juniper berries, lightly crushed

Salt and freshly ground black pepper

1 lb red cabbage, outer leaves and hard central core discarded

1 Using the Rotor Slicer/Shredder, with the slicing cone attached, on speed 4, slice the onion and apple into the bowl, then transfer to a heavy-base saucepan. Add the remaining ingredients, except for the cabbage, and bring to a boil.

2 Meanwhile slice the red cabbage through the slicing cone, on speed 4, and wash in plenty of cold water. Drain thoroughly, add to the saucepan and return to boiling.

3 Cover with the lid and reduce to a simmer, then cook for about 1 hour 30 minutes. While the cabbage cooks, take care not to allow the liquid to evaporate completely – top up with apple juice or red wine, and turn the heat down if necessary. Cook until tender, stirring frequently, and serve hot with meats or stews.

BRAISED CELERY HEARTS
A simple dish to prepare as a perfect accompaniment to white fish, celery hearts bring the flavor of French bistros to the table. If your celery is on the large side, break off the stalks, remove the strings with a vegetable peeler, and cut them into 2-inch lengths.

SERVES 4

Preparation time: 10 minutes

Cooking time: 45 minutes

Attachments used

1 carrot, peeled

1 onion, peeled

5 or 6 celery hearts

4 Tbsp butter

Salt and freshly ground black pepper

2 cups vegetable or chicken broth

1 bouquet garni (thyme, rosemary, and parsley)

1 Using the Rotor Slicer/Shredder, with the coarse shredding cone attached, on speed 4, slice the carrot and onion and chop into a bowl.

2 Remove the outer stalks of the celery to reveal the hearts. Keep them whole, removing just the leaves and the woody parts.

3 Rinse the celery hearts and blanch them for 5 minutes in well-salted boiling water. Drain and cool immediately in cold water.

4 Preheat the oven to 350ºF. Melt the butter in a saucepan over a low heat. Add the carrot and onion and fry them gently until they are soft, but not colored. Add the celery, season, and cover with the broth. Add the bouquet garni, cover, and place in the oven. After 20 minutes, turn the celery and return to the oven for a further 20 minutes. Serve hot.

NAPKIN DUMPLINGS (Serviettenknödel) A simple Central European dumpling made from tiny bits of bread soaked in

milk and steamed with onion. Serve as a side dish with winter stews, country soups, or braised red cabbage (see opposite).

SERVES 4

Preparation time: 20 minutes plus 30 minutes soaking time

Cooking time: 1 hour 20 minutes

Attachments used

6 crusty bread rolls

2 eggs

$1/2$ cup milk

$1/4$ tsp salt

1 onion, cut into 8 wedges

4 Tbsp butter

Handful fresh parsley leaves, chopped fine

Pinch of grated nutmeg

Freshly ground black pepper

1 Preheat the oven to 250°F. Cut the bread rolls into $1/2$-inch cubes or tear into tiny pieces. Put on a cookie sheet and bake for 20 minutes, turning occasionally until dry. Tip them into a large bowl.

2 Whisk the eggs, milk, and salt together. Slowly pour the mixture over the bread and gently stir to ensure the pieces are evenly coated.

3 Using the Rotor Slicer/Shredder with the coarse shredding cone attached, on speed 4, grate the onion into the bowl and set aside.

4 Melt the butter in a skillet and gently cook the onion for 10 to 15 minutes until soft. Add the parsley and cook for another minute. Remove from the heat and allow to cool for a few minutes, then add to the bread. Season with nutmeg and pepper and mix thoroughly, then cover, and leave in a cool place for at least 30 minutes to soak.

5 Shape the mixture into a roll, about 4 inches long. Place it on a clean, wet dish towel and roll up the cloth to enclose the mixture like a large sausage. Leave a little room at the ends for the dumpling to expand, then tie up in the middle and both ends with string.

6 Slide a wooden spoon through the string and hang the dumpling over a pot of boiling lightly salted water, covering just over half of the dumpling. Cover with a lid and gently simmer for 30 minutes. Carefully turn the dumpling over, so that the top side is now in the water, and cook for a further 25 minutes.

7 Remove from the water and leave it to stand for 5 minutes. To serve, carefully unwrap the dumpling and cut it into thick slices.

GRATIN DAUPHINOIS
A French dish of potatoes in cream, baked until a golden crust forms. To make boulangère potatoes, substitute a quarter of the potatoes for sliced onions, cover with vegetable broth, then dot with butter before baking.

SERVES 6

Preparation time: 15 minutes

Cooking time: 1 hour 15 minutes

Attachments used

2 lb potatoes

Butter

2 cloves garlic, chopped

2 oz Gruyère cheese

Salt and freshly ground black pepper

1/2 cup heavy cream (whipping cream)

2 cups milk

1 Preheat the oven to 350°F. With the slicing cone on the Rotor Slicer/Shredder, on speed 4, slice the potatoes. Using the fine shredding cone, shred the Gruyère.

2 Generously butter an ovenproof dish. Put the potatoes into the dish and tuck pieces of garlic and shredded Gruyère in amongst them. Season well. Mix the cream and milk together, and pour over the potatoes – it should come just to the top of the potatoes. Sprinkle Gruyère over the top.

3 Cover with foil and bake in the oven for about 1 hour 15 minutes, until the potatoes are tender. Remove the foil cover for the last 15 minutes of cooking time, to form a golden-brown crust.

ROSTI WITH APPLE SAUCE
Hot potato pancakes make a great accompaniment to sausages and roasted or broiled meats, or they can be served on their own as a snack with a spoonful of apple sauce.

SERVES 6

Preparation time: 10 minutes

Cooking time: 20 minutes

Attachments used

6 large waxy potatoes, such as Maris Piper

1 onion, cut into wedges

1 clove garlic (optional)

4 Tbsp all-purpose flour

2 eggs, beaten

Salt and freshly ground black pepper

4 Tbsp unsalted butter

4 Tbsp oil

For the apple sauce

8 oz tart apples (such as Granny Smith), peeled and cored

8 oz dessert apples, peeled and cored

3 Tbsp superfine sugar

2 Tbsp water

1 Place a strainer over the mixer bowl. Using the Rotor Slicer/Shredder with the coarse shredding cone attached, on speed 4, shred the potatoes into the strainer. Press as much liquid out of the potatoes as possible. Discard the liquid and tip the potatoes into the bowl.

2 Change to the medium shredding cone and, still on speed 4, shred the onion and garlic into the bowl. Sprinkle over the flour, then add the eggs. Season with salt and pepper, and mix well.

3 To make the apple sauce, use the slicing cone to slice the apples into a saucepan. Add the sugar and water. Cover and simmer for 15 minutes. Stir occasionally during cooking. Beat with a fork and set aside.

4 Heat half the butter and half the oil together in a large skillet, then add large spoonfuls of the potato mixture to form rounds. Flatten the pancakes with the back of a dampened spoon.

5 Fry the pancakes over a medium heat until dark golden brown and crisp, then turn over and cook on the other side. Drain on paper towels and keep warm while cooking the rest of the pancakes, adding more butter and oil to the pan when needed. Serve hot with the apple sauce.

SWEET CUCUMBER PICKLE
This sweet pickle can be stuffed into whole grain sandwiches with cheese or carved leg ham and salad, or served on the side with hamburgers or hot dogs.

MAKES 2¹/₂ CUPS

Preparation time: 20 minutes plus 2 hours standing time

Cooking time: 25 minutes

Attachments used

3 large onions

3 large cucumbers, unpeeled

2 tsp fine sea salt

2¹/₄ cups superfine sugar

2¹/₂ cups white wine vinegar

1 Tbsp mustard seeds

1. With the slicing cone on the Rotor Slicer/Shredder, on speed 4, slice the onions and the cucumbers.

2. In a large colander layer the vegetables, sprinkling the salt between the layers. Place a plate on top and press down with a heavy weight. Leave for at least 2 hours, then squeeze out as much of the remaining liquid as possible.

3. In a large pan, stir the sugar into the vinegar with the mustard seeds until the sugar has dissolved completely. Bring slowly to a boil.

4. Add the drained vegetables and again bring to a boil. Simmer, uncovered, for 1 minute. Remove from the heat and drain the vegetables, reserving the liquid, then spoon into hot, sterilized jars. Return the liquid to the pan and boil for a further 15 minutes, uncovered, then pour over the onion and cucumber in the jars. Seal when completely cold.

PEACH CHUTNEY
Similar to India's mango chutney, this peach chutney is a wonderful accompaniment to spicy curries, as well as a great partner for cold meats or bread and cheese.

MAKES 5 CUPS

Preparation time: 20 minutes

Cooking time: 2 hours

Attachments used

12 firm peaches, halved and pitted

3 red bell peppers, deseeded and quartered

1 large onion, halved

3/4 cup cider vinegar

3/4 cup sugar

1/2 clove garlic, minced

1/2 tsp salt

1/2 cup raisins

1/2 navel orange, peeled, deseeded, and quartered

1/2 lemon, peeled, deseeded, and quartered

2 Tbsp chopped crystallized ginger

1/2 tsp ground ginger

1 With the slicing cone on the Rotor Slicer/Shredder, on speed 4, slice the peaches, peppers, and onion thick and set aside.

2 Heat 1/2 cup of the vinegar and the sugar in a 10-pint pot over a medium heat. Bring the mixture to a boil, then reduce the heat, and simmer for 10 minutes.

3 Add the peach, peppers, onion, garlic, salt, and raisins to the pot. Simmer, stirring frequently, for 10 minutes.

4 Using the food grinder, with the coarse grinding plate attached, on speed 4, grind the orange and lemon. Add the pulped fruit and crystallized ginger to the pot and simmer for 30 minutes, stirring occasionally.

5 Add the remaining vinegar and ground ginger to the mixture. Simmer for 1 hour or until thick, stirring occasionally. Ladle the mixture into hot, sterilized jars and seal them. Place in a saucepan of boiling water and simmer for 15 minutes. Remove the jars from the bath, then cool them and check the seals.

ZUCCHINI AND TOMATO SAUTÉ
You can, if preferred, use marrow or any other squash for this recipe. If using squashes such as acorn or butternut squash, ensure that they are young and tender when you buy them.

SERVES 4

Preparation time: 10 minutes

Cooking time: 20 minutes

Attachments used

1 onion

1–2 cloves garlic

1 lb zucchini

2 Tbsp unsalted butter

14-oz can chopped tomatoes

Salt and freshly ground black pepper

1 Tbsp chopped fresh oregano

4 oz feta cheese, diced (optional)

1 With the slicing cone on the Rotor Slicer/Shredder, on speed 4, slice the onion, garlic, and zucchini separately. Heat the butter in a large skillet, then sauté the onion and garlic for 3 minutes. Add the zucchini and continue to sauté for 2 minutes.

2 Add the tomatoes, with seasoning to taste, and the chopped oregano, and bring to a boil, stirring occasionally. Reduce the heat, cover with either a lid or tinfoil, and simmer for 10 to 15 minutes or until the vegetables are tender. Adjust the seasoning and add the cheese if using.

ZUCCHINI WITH GARLIC
A classic partnership of zucchini with a little garlic. Instead of shredding the zucchini, you could use the slicing cone to slice them thin, then cook in the same way.

SERVES 2

Preparation time: 10 minutes

Cooking time: 10 minutes

Attachments used

2 medium or 4 small zucchini

2 cloves garlic, chopped fine

Olive oil

Salt and freshly ground black pepper

1 Shred the zucchini, using the coarse shredding cone on the Rotor Slicer/Shredder, on speed 4.

2 Put the garlic in a pan in which a small quantity of olive oil has been heated. When the garlic starts to give off its aroma, but before it turns brown, tip in the zucchini.

3 Cook over a moderate heat for 5 to 10 minutes, until the zucchini are just cooked. Season and serve.

LEEK AND ZUCCHINI QUICHE
A vegetarian quiche made with a classic shortcrust pastry that combines lard and butter for both texture and flavor. Choose small leeks with tender green tops as these are the sweetest when cooked.

SERVES 4 TO 6

Preparation time: 30 minutes, plus 30 minutes chilling

Cooking time: 45 minutes

Attachments used

For the pastry

2 cups all-purpose flour

Pinch of salt

4 Tbsp butter

1 Tbsp lard

1/2 cup iced water

For the filling

4 Tbsp butter

3 leeks, sliced

1 zucchini, sliced

1 clove garlic, crushed

4 eggs

2 Tbsp plain yogurt

1/2 cup milk

4 oz Gruyère or mature Cheddar cheese, shredded

Salt and freshly ground black pepper

1 Preheat the oven to 375°F. Sift the flour and salt into the mixer bowl. Cut the butter and lard into cubes and add to the flour. Using the flat beater, on speed 2, beat until well blended. Add enough iced water to make a smooth dough, then shape into a ball, wrap in plastic wrap, and chill in the refrigerator for 30 minutes.

2 To make the filling, heat the butter in a pan. Gently fry the leek, zucchini, and garlic until soft. Remove from the heat.

3 Mix the eggs, yogurt, milk, cheese, and some salt and pepper thoroughly in a bowl.

4 Roll the dough out thin and line an 8-inch baking pan. Add the leek and zucchini filling and pour in the cheese mixture. Smooth it over on top.

5 Bake in the oven for about 45 minutes until the quiche is firm and golden brown. Garnish with salad leaves and serve hot or cold.

SPINACH AND CHEESE SOUFFLÉ

French soufflés are not as difficult to make as their reputation implies – in fact, the hardest part can be ensuring that everyone is assembled when the soufflé is brought to the table so they can appreciate how well it has risen.

SERVES 4

Preparation time: 45 minutes

Cooking time: 50 minutes

Attachments used

1¹/₄ cups fresh spinach, washed thoroughly

4 oz mature Cheddar cheese

4 Tbsp unsalted butter

¹/₃ cup all-purpose flour

1 cup warm milk

4 medium eggs, separated

1 tsp Dijon mustard

Salt and freshly ground black pepper

1 Preheat the oven to 350°F. Lightly butter a 2-pint (8-inch diameter) soufflé dish. Place a cookie sheet in the oven to heat. Place the spinach, with just the water clinging to the leaves, into a saucepan and cook for 3 to 4 minutes or until wilted. Drain thoroughly and chop fine, then place in paper towels and squeeze out any excess moisture.

2 With the coarse shredding cone on the Rotor Slicer/Shredder, on speed 4, shred the cheese.

3 Melt the butter in a saucepan and stir in the flour, cook over a gentle heat for 2 minutes, then take the pan off the heat, and gradually stir in the warm milk. Return to the heat and stir for 2 minutes, or until the mixture thickens and coats the back of the spoon. Remove from the heat and place in the mixer bowl.

4 Cool slightly, then with the flat beater, at speed 6, beat in the egg yolks one at a time, beating well between each addition. When all the egg yolks have been added, stir in the spinach and all but 1 tablespoon of the cheese, along with the mustard and some seasoning. Stir until the cheese has melted. Pour into another bowl.

5 Clean the mixer bowl and dry thoroughly, then add the egg whites and, using the wire whip, on speed 10, whisk until stiff and standing in peaks. Stir 1 tablespoon into the cheese mixture, then gently stir in the remaining egg whites.

6 Spoon the mixture into the prepared dish, place on the hot cookie sheet, and cook undisturbed in the oven for 50 minutes, or until well risen and golden brown. Serve immediately.

BREADS

GRANARY AND WALNUT BREAD
Granary flour is a mixture of white, whole wheat, and rye flours blended with malted grains. The flour gives a nutty taste that complements the walnuts in this country bread.

MAKES 2 LOAVES

Preparation time: 15 minutes plus standing time

Cooking time: 40 minutes

Attachments used

8 cups granary or other less refined flour

2 tsp salt

1 heaping tsp active dry yeast

$^3/_4$ cup walnuts, roughly chopped

2 Tbsp oil

About $2^1/_2$ cups tepid water

1   Preheat the oven to 425°F. Place the flour, salt, yeast, and nuts into the mixer bowl. Using the flat beater, on speed 2, mix the dry ingredients for a few seconds.

2   Change to the dough hook and, on speed 2 again, gradually add the oil and the tepid water. If the mixture looks at all dry, add a little more water until it looks moist. Knead for about 1 minute only on this speed. Place in a greased bowl, turning the dough over once to grease the top. Cover and leave to rise in a warm, draft-free place for about 1 hour, or until doubled in bulk.

3   Knead well again, adding a little extra flour if the dough seems too sticky. The machine may be stopped once or twice and the dough pulled away from hook. Divide into two and place in two greased 2-pound loaf pans. Cover and leave to rise in a warm place, free from drafts, for about 1 hour, or until risen well above the tops of the pans.

4   Bake in the oven for 10 minutes, then reduce the heat to 400°F for another 30 minutes. The loaves are cooked when, turned out of their pans, they sound hollow if tapped on the base. Cool on a wire rack.

When making bread add the liquids gradually so they do not form a pool around the dough hook and slow down the mixing process.

The KitchenAid mixer will really start to knead the bread when the dough begins to cling to the dough hook, and you can then continue kneading until the dough is smooth.

PAIN DE CAMPAGNE

(Country bread) A coarse French loaf made from a mixture of buckwheat, rye, and white flours.

This everyday bread keeps well and makes great toast.

MAKES 2 SMALL LOAVES

Preparation time: 15 minutes plus 1 hour 45 minutes rising time

Cooking time: 40 minutes

Attachments used

$1^2/_3$ cups buckwheat flour

$1^2/_3$ cups rye flour

3 cups white bread flour

2 tsp salt

1 heaping tsp active dry yeast

1 Tbsp clear honey

1 cup warm water

2 Tbsp melted butter

$^2/_3$ cup strong dark beer, such as Guinness

1 Put the flours, salt, and yeast in the mixer bowl and blend with the dough hook on speed 1 for a few seconds.

2 Stir the honey into the water until mixed together, then add the melted butter and beer, and mix again.

3 Using the dough hook on speed 2, gradually add the beer mixture to the bowl and blend to a smooth dough. Continue kneading with the dough hook on speed 2 for 5 to 6 more minutes, until the dough is smooth and elastic.

4 Cover the bowl with plastic wrap and leave the dough to rise in a warm, draft-free place for about an hour, or until doubled in bulk.

5 Punch the dough down, then divide into two, and shape each half into a round loaf. Transfer to a greased cookie sheet, cover with oiled plastic wrap, and leave to rise for a further 45 minutes, or until doubled in size.

6 Meanwhile, preheat the oven to 425°F. Lightly dust the tops of the loaves with flour, then slash in a criss-cross pattern with a sharp knife.

7 Bake for 10 minutes, then lower the heat to 400°F and bake for a further 25 to 30 minutes, until the loaves are risen and sound hollow when tapped underneath.

TOMATO AND OLIVE OIL BREAD
Similar in preparation to traditional focaccia, yet much faster, this olive oil bread is enlivened with sweet tomatoes and garlic. It's delicious served with fresh goat cheese and a salad.

MAKES 1 LARGE LOAF

Preparation time: 30 minutes plus 2 hours 20 minutes rising time

Cooking time: 30 minutes

Attachments used

4 cups white bread flour

1 Tbsp salt

1 heaping tsp active dry yeast

1/2 cup olive oil

1 1/2 cups lukewarm water

12 cherry tomatoes, halved

1 to 2 cloves garlic, sliced very fine

Olive oil and coarse sea salt, for topping

1 Blend the flour, salt, and yeast together on speed 2 using the dough hook, then add the olive oil and most of the water. Mix, and knead thoroughly, still on speed 2, adding enough water to make a soft but manageable dough. The kneading will take about 5 to 6 minutes.

2 Scrape the dough off the hook back into the bowl. Cover with plastic wrap and leave in a warm, draft-free place for two hours until well risen.

3 Knead the dough again, with the dough hook on speed 2, until the dough returns to its original size. Turn out onto a lightly floured surface.

4 Generously oil a small rectangular roasting pan, about 8 x 10 inches. Divide the dough in half and roll out one piece to roughly fit the base of the pan, stretching it into the corners. Cover with the halved tomatoes and garlic, and season lightly with salt and pepper. Roll out the remaining dough and place it over the tomatoes. Cover the pan with plastic wrap and leave in a warm, draft-free place again for about 20 minutes, until just starting to rise.

5 Preheat the oven to 425°F. Carefully make indentations all over the dough with your fingertips to seal the two halves together and stop the dough from rising too much. Drizzle with a little olive oil and sprinkle with coarse sea salt, then bake for 25 to 30 minutes until golden brown. Cool on a wire rack before serving.

PITA BREAD
This Middle-Eastern flatbread can be cooked in the oven or on a griddle or open fire. It puffs up to leave a pocket that can be stuffed with a sandwich filling or torn open to scoop up a spicy dip.

MAKES 6 PITA BREADS

Preparation time: 30 minutes plus 2 hours standing time

Cooking time: 30 minutes

Attachments used

1 cup whole wheat flour

3 1/2 cups all-purpose flour

1 Tbsp sugar

2 tsp salt

1 heaping tsp active dry yeast

2 cups very warm water

1 Tbsp olive oil

1 Mix the flours together and place 4 cups of this mixture in the mixer bowl, with the sugar, salt, and yeast. Using the dough hook, on speed 2, mix for 15 seconds. Gradually add the warm water and olive oil, and mix for 1 minute. Continuing on speed 2, add the remaining flour mixture, 1/3 cup at a time, until the dough cleans the sides of the bowl. Knead on speed 2 for 2 minutes longer, or until the dough is smooth and elastic.

2 Cover and leave to rise in a warm, draft-free place for about 1 hour, or until doubled in bulk. Preheat the oven to 475°F.

3 Punch the dough down and divide into six equal pieces. Roll each piece into a 7-inch circle, and place on foil to rise, uncovered, at room temperature for 1 hour. Bake for 5 to 6 minutes. Cool on a wire rack.

SOURDOUGH

Sourdough is made from a starter that can be refrigerated and used as needed. Stir $1/2$ cup water and 1 cup white bread flour into the remaining starter from the recipe below, and leave to ferment at room temperature for 12 to 24 hours before refrigerating.

MAKES 1 LOAF

Preparation time: 20 minutes plus 2 hours rising and 2 to 3 days fermenting time

Cooking time: 40 minutes

For the starter
2$1/4$ cups white bread flour
1 heaping tsp active dry yeast
1$1/4$ cups water

For the dough
3$1/4$ cups white bread flour
1$1/2$ tsp salt
1 tsp active dry yeast
$3/4$ cup tepid water

Attachments used

1 To make the starter, sift the flour into the mixer bowl and stir in the yeast. Add the water and stir together with the flat beater. Pour into a bowl, cover loosely, and keep in a warm draft-free place. The mixture is ready to use when it has a pleasant sour smell, between 2 and 3 days. Stir it twice daily.

2 To make the dough, sift the flour and salt into the mixer bowl and stir in the yeast. Measure 1 cup of the starter into a jug, reserving the remaining starter, then stir in the tepid water. Using the dough hook, on speed 1, gradually add the starter mixture and blend to a smooth dough. Continue kneading on speed 2 for another 3 minutes, until smooth and elastic.

3 Cover the bowl with plastic wrap and leave the dough to rise in a warm draft-free place for about an hour, until doubled in size. Knock back, then leave to rest for 10 minutes.

4 Shape the dough into a round or long oval shape and place on a greased cookie sheet. Cover with oiled plastic wrap and leave to rise in a warm draft-free place for about an hour, or until doubled in size.

5 Place a tray of water on the bottom shelf of the oven, then preheat the oven to 425°F. Lightly dust the loaf with flour, then cut three parallel slashes about $1/4$ inch deep across the top of the loaf, and three more slashes in the opposite direction to make a criss-cross pattern.

6 Bake the loaf for 10 minutes, then reduce the heat to 400°F and bake for a further 30 minutes, or until golden and hollow-sounding when tapped on the bottom. Leave to cool on a wire rack.

FOCACCIA An Italian flatbread, traditionally toasted over an open fire and topped with olive oil and coarse salt.

There are many variations, and this one is made with mashed potatoes and covered with tomatoes and oregano.

SERVES 12

Preparation time: 10 minutes plus 3 hours proving time

Cooking time: 30 minutes

Attachments used

4¹/₂ cups white bread flour

2 cups cooked and mashed potatoes (page 80)

4 Tbsp olive oil

1 heaping tsp active dry yeast

2 eggs

1 tsp salt

For the topping

¹/₂ cup olive oil

15 small tomatoes, halved or quartered

2 Tbsp chopped fresh oregano or thyme

Pinch of salt

1   Preheat the oven to 350°F. Put the flour, mashed potatoes, olive oil, yeast, eggs, and salt into the mixer bowl. With the dough hook, mix the dough on speed 2 for 30 seconds. Increase to speed 4 and continue mixing until a smooth dough forms. Divide into two.

2   Lightly grease a two 8-inch round cake pans and shape the dough into the pan. Lightly cover the top and leave to rest for 3 hours until risen.

3   Brush the olive oil over the dough and arrange the tomato pieces on top. Sprinkle the oregano, or thyme, and salt on the tomatoes and cook in the oven for 30 minutes, covering lightly with foil halfway through cooking to prevent the topping from coloring. Serve warm.

PRETZELS
The original bar snack, pretzels originated in Germany and Austria but are now just as popular in America. They should be salty and hard on the outside, but have a chewy interior.

MAKES 10 TO 12 PRETZELS

Preparation time: 15 minutes, plus 15 minutes standing time

Cooking time: 30 minutes

Attachments used

4^{1}/$_{4}$ cups all-purpose flour

Pinch of salt

1 Tbsp active dry yeast

^{1}/$_{4}$ cup sugar

6 Tbsp shortening

^{1}/$_{2}$ cup tepid milk

^{1}/$_{4}$ cup all-purpose flour, for dusting

^{1}/$_{2}$ cup salted warm water, for brushing

1 Tbsp coarse salt, for sprinkling

1   Preheat the oven to 425ºF. Put the flour, pinch of salt, yeast, sugar, and the lard in the mixer bowl. Using the dough hook on speed 1, mix in the tepid milk until the mixture forms a dough. Cover and leave to rest in a warm, draft-free place for 15 minutes.

2   Using the dough hook on speed 1, knead again to make a supple but firm dough that is elastic and leaves the sides of the bowl clean.

3   Dust your hands with the flour and make 15-inch long rolls of dough, about ^{1}/$_{2}$ inch in diameter. Turn both ends of each roll inwards into a loose knot shape.

4   Place the pretzels on a greased cookie sheet. Brush with the salted water and sprinkle them with salt, very gently pressing the salt grains into the dough.

5   Bake in the oven for 30 minutes, brushing the pretzels with the salted water twice again during baking so they are nice and crisp. Allow to cool, then store the pretzels in an airtight container.

CHAPATI
A circular flatbread made in India and Pakistan from a fine whole wheat chapati flour, called atta, and water. This version uses whole wheat flour. Chapatis are used to scoop up curries.

MAKES 12 CHAPATIS

Preparation time: 15 minutes plus 30 minutes standing time

Cooking time: 30 minutes

Attachments used

3/4 cup water

2 1/4 cups whole wheat flour, sifted

Pinch of salt

Butter or oil, for brushing

1 In the mixer bowl, with the dough hook on speed 1, gradually add the water to the sifted flour and the salt to form a soft dough. It will be quite sticky. Knead for 4 to 5 minutes on speed 2. Cover with the plastic bowl cover and leave to rise in a warm, draft-free place for about 30 minutes.

2 Divide the dough into 12 pieces. Take one piece and roll into a ball, then flatten. Using a rolling pin and dusting well with flour, roll into a circle about 5 to 6 inches in diameter.

3 Shake off any excess flour and put the chapati onto a preheated cast-iron flat griddle or skillet. Cook on a low heat for 1 to 2 minutes. Turn the chapati over and cook on the other side.

4 Brush a little melted butter or some oil over the surface of the chapati and eat while fresh. Make the rest of the chapatis in the same way.

STOLLEN
These traditional sweet loaves are found all over northern Europe in the winter, although they originate in Germany. Tie the baked stollen with a ribbon to make a charming gift for friends at Christmas time.

MAKES 2 LOAVES

Preparation time: 2 hours plus 2 hours 30 minutes standing time

Cooking time: 30 minutes

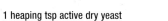

Attachments used

1 heaping tsp active dry yeast

1 tsp superfine sugar

4$\frac{1}{4}$ cups all-purpose flour

$\frac{2}{3}$ cup lukewarm milk

Pinch of salt

3 Tbsp light brown sugar or light Muscovado sugar, if available

4 Tbsp butter, cut into slices

2 eggs, beaten

1 Tbsp rum

1 cup mixed dried fruit

Grated rind of half a lemon

5 oz marzipan or almond paste

Butter, for glazing

Confectioners' sugar, for dredging

1 Stir the yeast, superfine sugar, 1 cup of the flour, and the milk together in the mixer bowl, using the flat beater. Cover and leave in a warm place for at least an hour, until it starts to become frothy.

2 Add the remaining flour, salt, brown sugar, butter, most, but not all, of the beaten eggs, and the rum and mix to a manageable dough with the dough hook on speed 4, adding a little extra milk if necessary. Knead thoroughly with the dough hook on speed 4 for 5 minutes, then cover, and leave in a warm, draft-free place for an hour, or until doubled in bulk.

3 Knead the dough lightly, then gently work in the dried fruit and lemon rind using the dough hook on speed 4, do not overknead. Turn out onto a lightly floured surface and divide into two. Shape into ovals, about $\frac{1}{2}$ inch thick.

4 Roll the marzipan into two even lengths to fit the length of the loaves. Press the rolling pin into the dough to make an indentation about one-third of the way from the bottom of each oval. Lay the marzipan in the marked places, then fold the dough over towards you, leaving the ends of the marzipan just showing if possible. Seal the edges with some of

the remaining beaten egg. Place the loaves on a lightly buttered cookie sheet, cover, and leave to rise again for about 30 minutes.

5 Preheat the oven to 350°F. Brush the dough with any remaining egg and bake for 30 minutes, or until golden brown.

6 Cool on a wire rack. Melt a little extra butter, brush over the cooled loaves, and top with sifted confectioners' sugar.

PANETTONE
This light and buttery cake-like bread from Milan is traditionally eaten over Christmas and Easter. Do not add more than the amount of flour specified or the panettone will be dry.

MAKES 1 LOAF

Preparation time: 40 minutes plus 2 hours standing time

Cooking time: 1 hour

Attachments used

1 heaping tsp active dry yeast

1 cup warm milk

4 cups all-purpose flour

1 tsp salt

1/2 cup raisins

1 tsp grated lemon peel

3/4 cup chopped citron or candied peel

1/4 cup sugar

1/2 cup vegetable oil

4 Tbsp butter, melted

4 egg yolks

1 egg white

1 Tbsp water

1. Preheat the oven to 350°F. Dissolve the yeast in the warm milk. Place 3 cups of the flour, the salt, raisins, lemon peel, citron, and sugar in the mixer bowl. Using the dough hook, on speed 2, mix for 15 seconds. Add the oil and butter to the mixture.

2. On speed 2, gradually add the warm milk and yeast and the egg yolks to the mixer bowl and mix for 1 minute. Continuing on speed 2, add the remaining flour, 1/2 cup at a time, until the dough clings to the hook and cleans the sides of the bowl. Knead on speed 2 for 2 minutes longer.

3. Place in a greased bowl, turning the dough over once to grease the top. Cover and leave to rise in a warm, draft-free place for about 1 hour, or until doubled in bulk.

4. Punch the dough down and shape into a ball. Place in a greased 31/2-pint (12-inch diameter) soufflé dish. Leave to rise, but this time uncovered, in a warm, draft-free place for a further hour, until doubled in bulk.

5. Cut two slashes with a sharp knife in a cross pattern on the top of the loaf. Beat the egg white and water together with a fork and brush the top of the loaf with this mixture. Bake the loaf in the oven for 55 to 60 minutes.

6. When cooked, remove the loaf from the baking dish immediately and allow to cool on a wire rack.

SWEET BRAIDED ROLLS (Flachswickel) Little German rolls, made with lots of butter, coated in confectioners' sugar, and braided. Serve warm at breakfast time with homemade fruit jam or some honey.

MAKES 8

Preparation time: 15 minutes plus 1 hour rising time

Cooking time: 20 minutes

Attachments used

1¹/₂ sticks butter (6 oz)

²/₃ cup milk

4¹/₄ cups all-purpose flour

1 heaping tsp active dry yeast

2 Tbsp superfine sugar

2 eggs

Pinch of salt

2 Tbsp confectioners' sugar, sifted

1 Put the butter and milk into a small saucepan and heat gently to melt. When melted, pour into the mixer bowl with the flour, yeast, sugar, eggs, and salt. With the dough hook, mix on speed 4 for 3 minutes until combined. Cover and leave in a warm, draft-free place for 30 minutes.

2 Preheat the oven to 325ºF. Remove the dough from the mixer bowl and divide into 24 equal-size pieces. Roll each piece into a sausage shape and roll them in the confectioners' sugar.

3 Lay three pieces of dough side by side and press the ends of these together. Braid the three pieces, pressing the other ends together to finish. Repeat with the remaining dough to make eight rolls. Transfer to a cookie sheet and leave to stand for 30 minutes. Cook the rolls in the oven for 20 minutes until golden brown, and serve warm.

LEMON BRIOCHE
A cake-like French bread made with eggs and butter and flavored here with lemon. It puffs up to form a loaf that is perfect for a light breakfast, served warm with butter and jam.

MAKES ONE 1-lb LOAF

Preparation time: 25 minutes plus 2 hours

10 minutes rising time

Cooking time: 30 minutes

Attachments used

2 Tbsp superfine sugar

3 Tbsp water

1 heaping tsp active dry yeast

2 eggs

1^2/$_3$ cups all-purpose flour

^{1}/$_4$ tsp salt

Grated rind of 1 lemon

1 stick unsalted butter (¼ lb), cubed

1 egg yolk, to glaze

1 Tbsp water, to glaze

1 Put 1 tablespoon of sugar in a small saucepan with the water and dissolve the sugar over a low heat. Sprinkle the yeast onto the mixture and leave to stand for 5 to 10 minutes until frothy. Stir the yeast into the liquid and beat in the eggs.

2 Put the flour, salt, lemon rind, and remaining sugar into the mixer bowl and, with the dough hook, blend the ingredients on speed 1.

3 Increasing to speed 3, gradually add the yeast mixture to form a dough and then knead for a further 2 to 3 minutes, scraping the dough down the sides of the bowl as required. Add the butter to the mixture, mixing on speed 6 for 3 minutes until fully combined.

4 Put the dough in a large oiled bowl, cover with a clean damp dish towel, and leave to rise in a warm, draft-free place for 1 hour 30 minutes until doubled in bulk.

5 Grease a 1-lb pan with butter. Knead the dough two or three times on a lightly floured board and divide into eight even-size pieces. Roll each piece into a ball and place in the pan. Cover and leave to prove for 40 minutes.

6 Preheat the oven to 400°F. Mix the egg yolk and water to form a glaze and brush over the top of the dough. Cook in the oven for 30 minutes until the loaf is golden brown. Unmold the loaf immediately and serve warm with butter and jam.

CROISSANTS
If the butter oozes out of this rich, French pastry dough while you are rolling and folding, slide the dough onto a cookie sheet and chill until it is easier to handle.

MAKES 12

Preparation time: 30 minutes plus 1 hour chilling and 2 hours rising time

Cooking time: 15 minutes

Attachments used

3 cups all-purpose flour

$^1/_2$ tsp salt

1 Tbsp superfine sugar

1 heaping tsp active dry yeast

$^1/_3$ cup near-boiling water

$^1/_3$ cup milk

1$^1/_2$ sticks unsalted butter (6 oz)

1 egg, beaten

1 Sift the flour and salt into the mixer bowl. Add the sugar and yeast, and mix together for a few seconds with the dough hook on speed 1.

2 Mix the water and milk and check the temperature with your finger – it should be tepid. Still on speed 1, pour the liquid into a well in the flour and mix together. Then knead the dough on speed 2 for 2 minutes until smooth and elastic. Cover with plastic wrap and leave in a warm place to rise for about an hour, or until doubled in size

3 Punch down the dough and turn out onto a floured surface. Knead until smooth. Wrap in a dish towel and refrigerate for 10 minutes.

4 Put the butter between two sheets of plastic wrap and roll into a rectangle. Fold the butter in half and roll out again. Repeat until it is pliable, but still cold, then flatten to form it into a 6 x 4-inch rectangle.

5 On a floured surface, roll out the dough to a rectangle, about 12 x 6 inches. With one short side facing you, place the block of butter in the center. Fold the bottom third of the dough over the butter and then fold the top third down over the two. Press the open sides together to seal.

6 Half-turn the dough, clockwise. Roll out to a rectangle and repeat the folding process twice more, then wrap, and chill for 30 minutes. Repeat the rolling and folding process twice more. Chill for a final 30 minutes.

7 Dampen two cookie sheets with water. Roll the chilled dough to a rectangle, about 18 x 12 inches. Cut into six even-size squares, then cut each square in half diagonally.

8 Starting at the base of each triangle, roll up loosely, and secure the point with a little beaten egg. Arrange point-side down on the cookie sheets, curving the ends to form a crescent shape. Lightly brush with the beaten egg, then cover with oiled plastic wrap and leave to prove in a warm draft-free place for about one hour, or until doubled in size.

9 Preheat the oven to 450°F. Remove the plastic wrap and brush again with the egg glaze. Bake for 3 minutes, then lower the temperature to 375°F, and bake for a further 10 to 12 minutes, until golden and crisp. Leave on the cookie sheets for a few minutes, then transfer to a wire rack. Serve warm or cold.

VARIATIONS

ALMOND CROISSANTS – Using the flat beater, on speed 4, blend 3 tablespoons butter and $^1/_2$ cup superfine sugar together. Beat in 1 egg yolk and 1 cup ground almonds to make a thick paste. Place a tablespoonful of the paste about 1 inch up from the base of each triangle before rolling up the croissants. Scatter a few flaked almonds over the top before baking and serve lightly dusted with confectioners' sugar.

CHOCOLATE CROISSANTS – Using the Rotor Slicer/Shredder with the coarse shredding cone attached, on speed 4, shred 3 oz dark, milk, or white chocolate, and divide among the triangles of croissant dough, about 1 inch up from the base, then roll up as before.

DESSERTS AND DRINKS

PASTRIES
The KitchenAid mixer makes wonderful pastry because it does not overhandle the dough, keeping it cool and easy to work with. These four basic pastries can be used to make simple tarts or more elaborate desserts.

STRUDEL PASTRY
This is one pastry that doesn't need gentle handling – the more stretching and beating the better to develop the gluten in the flour. It isn't difficult to make, but you do need a large work surface to roll it out until almost transparent.

MAKES ABOUT 10 oz (enough for 1 large strudel)

Preparation time: 40 minutes plus 30 minutes resting time

Attachments used

2 cups white bread flour

1/2 tsp salt

1 egg, beaten

2 tsp sunflower oil

About 2/3 cup warm water

1 Sift the flour and salt into the mixer bowl and mix with the dough hook on speed 1. Stir the egg and oil into the water and with the machine still running, slowly add to the flour and mix to a soft, sticky dough.

2 Knead with the dough hook on speed 2 for 4 to 5 minutes until the dough is smooth and elastic. Cover the bowl with a dish towel or plastic wrap and leave the dough to rest for 30 minutes.

3 Lightly flour a very large clean cloth, such as a tablecloth. Roll out the dough very thin, lifting it frequently to prevent it sticking. Gently roll and stretch the dough with your hands until it forms a 24-inch square. Use a pair of sharp scissors to trim off the thick edges. Use straight away.

FLAKY PASTRY
Light, crisp, and buttery, flaky pastry is similar to puff pastry, but simpler. Instead of adding the fat in one piece, it is incorporated by dotting it over the rolled-out dough, creating pockets of air that help separate the many layers.

MAKES ABOUT 450 g

Preparation time: 20 minutes plus 2 hours chilling time

Attachments used

2 cups all-purpose or white bread flour

Pinch of salt

1 1/2 sticks chilled butter (6 oz), or half butter and half white vegetable fat or lard

2/3 cup chilled water

1 Sift the flour and salt into the mixer bowl. Cut 1/2 stick of the butter into cubes and scatter over the flour mixture, then using the flat beater on speed 2, blend until the mixture resembles bread crumbs.

2 Using the flat beater on speed 1, gradually pour the water into the bowl and mix to form a dough. Wrap in plastic wrap and chill for 30 minutes.

3 On a lightly floured surface, roll out the dough to a rectangle about 12 x 4 inches. Cut 3 tablespoons of the remaining butter into tiny pieces and dot them evenly all over the top two-thirds of the pastry, leaving a good margin around the edges.

4 Fold the bottom third of the pastry up and over the butter and then fold the top third of the dough down over the two. Press the open sides of the parcel together with the rolling pin to seal in the butter. Wrap in plastic wrap and chill for 10 minutes.

5 Give the dough a half turn, clockwise. Repeat the rolling and folding process, this time without adding any butter, then wrap and chill for 10 minutes. Roll out two more times, using 3 tablespoons butter each time. Wrap and chill again for 10 minutes. Roll out and fold again, without adding any butter. Wrap and chill for at least one hour, before using.

CHOUX PASTRY
Choux pastry puffs up to more than double its original size during baking to make a hollow center, which is perfect for stuffing with a sweet or savory filling.

MAKES ABOUT 5 oz

(enough for 20 small puffs or 12 éclairs)

Preparation time: 10 minutes

Attachments used

9 Tbsp all-purpose flour

Pinch of salt

4 Tbsp butter

$^2/_3$ cup water

2 eggs, beaten

1   Sift the flour and salt into a bowl or onto a sheet of waxed paper. Gently heat the butter and water in a saucepan until melted.

2   Increase the heat and as soon as the liquid is boiling fast, tip in all the flour and beat vigorously to form a smooth paste. Beat the mixture over a low heat until it begins to form a ball and leave the sides of the pan; this will take about 30 seconds.

3   Remove the pan from the heat and tip the mixture into the mixer bowl. Leave to cool for a minute or two.

4   Gradually add the eggs, beating well between each addition with the flat beater on speed 4, until you have a shiny paste. You may not need all the egg. The mixture is ready when it falls reluctantly from a spoon.

PÂTE SABLÉE
A rich, crisp-textured sweet pastry used mainly for tartlet and flan cases because it holds its shape well. The high proportion of sugar makes it softer than basic shortcrust pastry, so it needs to be well chilled before rolling and baking.

MAKES ABOUT 10 oz

(enough for a 9-inch flan dish or eight 3-inch tartlet pans)

Preparation time: 10 minutes plus 1 hour chilling time

Attachments used

$1^1/_4$ cups all-purpose flour

Pinch of salt

6 Tbsp chilled butter

$^1/_4$ cup confectioners' sugar

2 egg yolks

1 tsp chilled water

$^1/_2$ tsp vanilla extract (optional)

1   Sift the flour and salt into the mixer bowl. Cut the butter into cubes and scatter over the flour mixture, then using the flat beater on speed 2, blend until the mixture resembles bread crumbs.

2   Lift the beater and sift the confectioners' sugar over the flour mixture. Whisk together the egg yolks, water, and vanilla extract, if using, in a small bowl and sprinkle over the mixture.

3   Using the flat beater, blend for just a few seconds on speed 1 until the pastry begins to hold together. Test the dough by pinching a piece between your fingers; if it is still too crumbly add another teaspoon of chilled water and mix again.

4   Gather the dough together to form a ball, then knead on a lightly floured surface with just the heel of your hand for about a minute.

5   Shape the pastry back into a ball, then flatten into a flat round (this makes it easier when you start to roll it out). Wrap in plastic wrap and chill in the refrigerator for about an hour before using. If you store it in the refrigerator for longer, leave out at room temperature for about 10 minutes before rolling out.

PASTRY CREAMS All these pastry creams can be used to fill pastries, cakes, tarts, or choux buns.

The crème anglaise is a rich custard to pour over desserts. All can be flavored with vanilla, almond, or even chocolate.

CRÈME PÂTISSIÈRE (Confectioner's custard) This pastry cream is the classic filling for fruit-topped flans and tarts, and can

be piped into choux pastry buns. It's best made the day before so that it can be well-chilled before use.

MAKES ABOUT 1¹/₂ CUPS

(enough for an 8-inch pastry case)

Preparation time: 10 minutes plus 10 minutes

infusing time

Cooking time: 5 minutes

1¹/₄ cups milk

1 vanilla bean, split, or ¹/₂ tsp vanilla extract

3 egg yolks

¹/₄ cup superfine sugar

2 Tbsp all-purpose flour

2 Tbsp cornstarch

Attachments used

1 Pour the milk into a heavy-base saucepan, add the vanilla bean if using, and slowly bring to a boil. Take off the heat and leave to infuse for 10 minutes. Remove the vanilla bean.

2 Put the egg yolks and sugar in the mixer bowl and beat with the wire whip on speed 4 for 2 minutes or until very pale and thick. Gradually sift the flour and cornstarch over the creamed mixture and beat until blended.

3 Bring the milk back to boiling and slowly pour over the blended mixture, mixing with the wire whip on speed 1.

4 Pour the crème pâtissière into the saucepan and cook over a low heat, stirring with a wooden spoon until the mixture comes to a boil and thickens. Gently simmer for a minute, stirring all the time. Remove from the heat and stir in the vanilla extract, if using instead of the vanilla bean.

5 Transfer the crème pâtissière to a bowl and cover the surface with plastic wrap or a piece of damp waxed paper to prevent a skin forming as it cools.

CRÈME MOUSSELINE Crème mousseline is made by beating butter into crème pâtissière to give it a light, fluffy texture.

It is a delicious alternative to cream in éclairs and puff pastries as it retains its texture and won't soak into the pastry.

MAKES ABOUT 2¹/₄ CUPS

Preparation time: 10 minutes

¹/₄ cup superfine sugar

1 stick unsalted butter (¼ lb), at room temperature

1¹/₂ cups warm crème pâtissière (page 120)

Attachments used

1 Add the sugar and ¹/₄ stick of the butter to the crème pâtissière and stir until blended. Cover the surface with plastic wrap and leave to cool.

2 Put the remaining butter in the mixer bowl and beat with the flat beater on speed 4 for 2 minutes, or until pale.

3 On speed 1, beat in the cold crème pâtissière a tablespoon at a time with the flat beater, until the mixture is pale and fluffy. Use straight away, or cover and store in the refrigerator, then leave out at room temperature for 5 minutes before using.

CRÈME DESSERT
A sweet, thick cream made by adding egg yolks and superfine sugar to sour cream. Serve a spoonful with a cake, fruit flan, or hot baked fruit.

MAKES ABOUT 1 CUP

Preparation time: 5 minutes

Attachments used

4 egg yolks

3/4 cup superfine sugar

1/2 cup sour cream

1 Put the egg yolks and sugar in the mixer bowl and beat with the wire whip on speed 4 for 2 minutes, or until very pale and thick.

2 On speed 1, add the sour cream a tablespoon at a time, until just mixed, taking care not to overbeat or the crème dessert will lose its fluffy texture.

VARIATIONS

VANILLA CRÈME DESSERT – Add 1 teaspoon of vanilla extract with the sour cream.

CARAMEL CRÈME DESSERT – Use granulated brown sugar instead of superfine sugar.

CRÈME ANGLAISE
This thin egg custard can be served hot or chilled. Here it's made with the addition of a little cornstarch to reduce the risk of curdling, but you can leave it out if you prefer.

MAKES ABOUT 1 1/2 CUPS

Preparation time: 10 minutes plus 10 minutes infusing time

Cooking time: 5 minutes

Attachments used

1 1/4 cups milk, or a mixture of milk and light or heavy cream

1 vanilla bean, split, or 1/2 tsp vanilla extract

3 egg yolks

1 Tbsp superfine sugar

1 tsp cornstarch

1 Pour the milk into a heavy-base saucepan, add the vanilla bean if using, and bring slowly to a boil. Take off the heat, then leave to infuse for 10 minutes. Remove the vanilla bean.

2 Put the egg yolks, superfine sugar, and cornstarch in the mixer bowl. Beat with the wire whip on speed 2 until pale and thick.

3 Bring the milk back to boiling, then using the wire whip on speed 1, slowly pour into the egg and sugar mixture, and mix together.

4 Pour the mixture back into the saucepan, then cook over a low heat, stirring constantly until the custard thickens enough to lightly coat the back of a wooden spoon. Stir in the vanilla extract, if using.

5 Serve hot or cold. If serving cold, pour into a chilled bowl and cover the surface with plastic wrap or a piece of damp waxed paper to prevent a skin forming. Cool, then chill until ready to serve.

VARIATIONS

CITRUS CRÈME ANGLAISE – Infuse the milk with a finely pared strip of orange, lemon, or lime rind instead of vanilla.

CHOCOLATE CRÈME ANGLAISE – Melt 1/3 cup chopped dark chocolate with the milk.

CRÊPES (Pancakes) Thin, wispy French pancakes that can be eaten on their own with just a squeeze of lemon and sugar or filled with chicken, vegetables, or cheese, or something sweet, as here.

MAKES 10

Preparation time: 10 minutes

Cooking time: 35 minutes

Attachments used

1 cup all-purpose flour

1/4 cup superfine sugar

2 eggs

1 egg yolk

1/2 cup heavy cream (whipping cream)

1/2 cup milk

4 Tbsp butter

9 oz dessert apples, peeled, cored, and diced

2/3 cup raisins

Grated rind and juice of 1 lemon

3 Tbsp Calvados or other apple liqueur

Butter, for frying

Superfine sugar, for dredging

1 Sift the flour into the mixer bowl and add the sugar. With the wire whip on speed 1, gradually add the eggs, egg yolk, cream, and milk to make a batter. Mix for a further 1 minute on speed 4 to remove any lumps. Leave the batter to stand.

2 Meanwhile, put the butter into a saucepan with the diced apple, raisins, lemon juice and rind, and the Calvados. Cook over a medium heat for 5 to 7 minutes until the apples have softened.

3 Melt a little butter in a crêpe pan and pour off any excess. Spoon a tenth of the batter into the pan, swirling to coat the base with batter. Cook for 2 minutes until the underside is brown, flip the crêpe over, and cook for a further minute. Remove from the pan and keep the crêpe warm while cooking the remaining batter to make ten crêpes.

4 Spoon the apple filling into the center of each crêpe, roll the crêpes up, and sprinkle with superfine sugar. Serve warm.

BELGIAN WAFFLES
Waffles are made in a special waffle iron, which gives them their honeycombed appearance. Serve with maple syrup, ice cream, or confectioners' sugar and strawberries. They can also be eaten with bacon and maple syrup for breakfast.

MAKES 8

Preparation time: 15 minutes plus 1 hour standing time

Cooking time: 25 minutes

Attachments used

1^1/$_4$ cups milk

^{3}/$_4$ cup heavy cream (whipping cream)

2^1/$_4$ cups all-purpose flour

^{1}/$_4$ cup superfine sugar

1 tsp active dry yeast

4 eggs, separated

1^1/$_4$ sticks butter (5 oz), melted and cooled

Pinch of salt

Maple syrup, to serve (optional)

1 Warm the milk and cream to just below boiling point and set aside. Put the flour, 50 g of the sugar and the yeast in the mixer bowl. Using the flat beater, mix on speed 1 for 30 seconds. Stir in the egg yolks and mix on speed 2 for 2 minutes.

2 Add the milk and cream and the melted butter. Change to the wire whip and mix on speed 6 until a thick, smooth batter is formed. Transfer to a large bowl, cover and leave to stand at room temperature for 1 hour.

3 Clean the mixer bowl and the wire whip and dry thoroughly, then whisk the egg whites with a pinch of salt on speed 8 for 30 seconds until the egg whites are stiff. Add the remaining sugar and whisk again until peaking.

4 Fold the egg whites into the batter with a metal spoon and heat the waffle iron according to manufacturer's instructions. Pour enough batter into the iron to coat the base thinly, close the iron and cook for 2 to 3 minutes, turning the iron if it is not an electric model. The waffle is cooked when golden brown and crisp and it can be easily removed from the iron. Continue with the remaining batter and serve the waffles hot, with maple syrup.

EMPEROR PANCAKES (Kaiserschmarren) A fluffy pancake named after an Austrian Emperor and sprinkled with fried

raisins, a little sugar, and cinnamon just before serving.

SERVES 8

Preparation time: 10 minutes

Cooking time: 8 minutes

Attachments used

4 eggs

7 Tbsp butter

¹/₃ cup superfine sugar

Pinch of salt

³/₄ cup all-purpose flour

²/₃ cup milk

¹/₂ cup raisins

Oil, for frying

1 Tbsp superfine sugar, to sprinkle

¹/₂ tsp ground cinnamon, to sprinkle

1   Separate the eggs and put the whites into the mixer bowl. With the wire whip, whisk the egg whites for 1 minute on speed 8 until stiff and peaking. Remove from the mixer bowl and reserve.

2   Change to the flat beater, and put 4 tbsp of the butter, the sugar, and egg yolks into the bowl and blend these together, beginning on speed 4 and increasing to speed 6, for 1 minute. Blend in the salt, flour, and milk on speed 4 for 1 minute, then carefully mix in the egg whites.

3   Heat the remaining butter in a small pan and fry the raisins over a medium heat for 1 minute. Remove and set aside. Heat the oil in a large skillet, add the egg mixture, and cook over a medium heat for 4 to 5 minutes until cooked underneath and the center is set. Carefully flip the pancake over and cook for a further 3 to 4 minutes until cooked through.

4   Using two forks, cut the pancake into wedges and transfer to a warm serving plate. Sprinkle the raisins over the top with the sugar and ground cinnamon. Serve hot.

For recipes that require butter or margarine, you will need to use the flat beater rather than the wire whip to blend the ingredients, as fats can get stuck in the whip. It is very easy and quick to change the attachments, even in the middle of the recipe.

SWEET STEAMED DUMPLINGS (Dampfknödel) These German dumplings are cooked in a hot mixture

of sugar, butter, and water so that the hot top and bottom turn brown, while the middle stays white and soft. They are eaten here with a custard sauce.

SERVES 6

Preparation time: 20 minutes plus 50 minutes rising time

Cooking time: 50 minutes

Attachments used

1 cup milk

1 heaping tsp active dry yeast

$1/4$ cup superfine sugar

2 eggs

2 Tbsp vegetable oil

1 tsp salt

Grated rind of 1 lemon

$4 1/4$ cups white bread flour

2 Tbsp butter

For the custard sauce

2 eggs

1 Tbsp superfine sugar

1 cup milk

$1/2$ tsp vanilla extract

For cooking the dumplings

6 Tbsp butter

6 Tbsp superfine sugar

1 cup water

1 Warm the milk in a pan to lukewarm. Stir in the yeast and 1 teaspoon sugar, mixing until dissolved. Put the mixture in the mixer bowl and add the rest of the sugar, the eggs, oil, salt, lemon rind, 3 cups flour, and 2 tablespoons butter. With the dough hook, mix on speed 2 for 1 minute until a smooth, soft dough forms. Add any extra flour as required.

2 Knead the dough with the dough hook on speed 1 for 5 minutes until smooth. Transfer the dough to a lightly oiled bowl, cover, and leave to prove in a warm, draft-free place for 30 minutes until doubled in bulk.

3 Meanwhile, make the custard sauce by putting the eggs, sugar, and 3 tablespoons milk in the mixer bowl. Bring the remaining milk to a boil in a saucepan with the vanilla extract. Pour the milk on to the eggs and mix on speed 1 for 30 seconds using the flat beater. Transfer the

mixture to the saucepan and cook over a gentle heat until the mixture coats the back of a wooden spoon. Do not boil.

4 Shape the dough into 12 even-size balls and put on a cookie sheet lined with waxed paper. Cover and leave to prove for 15 to 20 minutes.

5 To cook the dumplings, put 2 tablespoons butter in a saucepan with 2 tablespoons sugar and a third of the water. Cover and bring to a boil. Add four dumplings at a time to the pan and cover. Reduce the heat and cook for 15 to 20 minutes. The dumplings fry when they are cooked and the water has evaporated. Remove them from the pan, keep warm, and repeat until all the dumplings are cooked, adding the same quantity of butter, sugar, and water to the pan for each batch. Serve with the custard sauce, and decorate with grated lemon rind.

FLOATING ISLANDS (Îles Flottantes) A light, French dessert of meringues floating in a crème anglaise sauce. You can
buy vanilla sugar, or make your own by keeping a vanilla bean in a jar of superfine sugar for at least two weeks before using.

SERVES 6

Preparation time: 20 minutes

Cooking time: 15 minutes plus 30 minutes chilling

Attachments used

3 eggs, separated

Pinch of salt

³/₄ cup vanilla sugar

2 cups milk

²/₃ cup light cream

1 Tbsp orange flower water (optional)

For the caramel

1 cup superfine sugar

3 Tbsp cold water

1 Using the wire whip on speed 6, beat the egg whites until frothy. Add the salt and beat on speed 8 until soft peaks form. Gradually add ¹/₂ cup of the vanilla sugar, a tablespoon at a time, beating well after each addition until the mixture is very stiff and shiny.

2 Pour the milk and cream into a wide saucepan and bring to a gentle simmer. Using two spoons, shape five or six ovals of meringue, carefully dropping them into the pan as you make them. Poach for 2 to 3 minutes, or until they have doubled in size and are firm.

3 Remove the meringues with a slotted spoon and drain on paper towels. Repeat with the remaining mixture – you should have about 18 meringues, depending on their size.

4 Put the egg yolks and the remaining vanilla sugar into the mixer bowl and beat with the wire whip on speed 4 until pale and creamy. Bring the milk and cream back to boiling, and with the wire whip on speed 1, slowly pour over the egg yolks.

5 Pour the mixture back into the pan and heat gently, stirring all the time, until the custard thickens slightly and coats the back of a wooden spoon, taking care not to boil it or it may curdle. Stir in the orange flower water, if using. Pour the custard into a serving dish and arrange the meringues on top. Cool, then chill for 30 minutes.

6 To make the caramel, put the sugar in a heavy-base saucepan with the water and heat gently until it is completely dissolved. Increase the heat and boil rapidly for a few minutes until a rich golden brown color, gently swirling the pan to ensure even coloring.

7 Carefully drizzle the caramel onto an oiled cookie sheet in zigzag patterns. Leave to cool and harden, then lift the caramel off, and use to decorate the meringues and custard. Serve straight away.

CHOCOLATE MOUSSE A classic rich French dessert, made even lighter by whisking the dark chocolate, cream, and eggs with the wire whip. Serve with a coulis or a crème anglaise and chocolate shavings.

SERVES 4

Preparation time: 15 minutes plus chilling time

Attachments used

8 oz bitter dark chocolate

1 Tbsp brandy or water

4 eggs, separated

3 Tbsp heavy cream (whipping cream)

1 Break the chocolate into squares and melt with the brandy or water in a double boiler or in a heatproof bowl over, but not touching, a saucepan of boiling water.

2 Put the melted chocolate and egg yolks in the mixer bowl and, with the wire whip, beat on speed 2 until thick and creamy.

3 Changing to speed 1 and still using the wire whip, add the cream until fully incorporated. Transfer the mixture to a large bowl.

4 Clean the mixer bowl and the wire whip and dry thoroughly, then whisk the egg whites with the wire whip on speed 8, until stiff and peaking. Fold into the chocolate mixture until well combined.

5 Spoon the mixture into serving dishes and chill for at least 1 hour before serving.

PLUM DUMPLINGS (Germknödel) A sweet Austrian dumpling enclosing a spoonful of plum jam and served with a sauce of vanilla butter. You can substitute any fruit jam you like for the plum jam. See note on Vanilla Sugar, Floating Islands (page 127)

MAKES 8

Preparation time: 20 minutes plus 1 hour 30 minutes standing time

Cooking time: 40 minutes

Attachments used

4 1/4 cups all-purpose flour

1 heaping tsp active dry yeast

1 cup warm milk

1 Tbsp superfine sugar

2 eggs

2 Tbsp butter, melted

1 tsp salt

3 drops lemon essence

8 tsp plum jam

1 Tbsp vanilla sugar

2 Tbsp butter

1 Sift the flour into the mixer bowl and make a well in the center. Add the yeast, 5 tablespoons milk, the sugar, eggs, melted butter, salt, and lemon essence. With the dough hook, mix on speed 2 for 30 seconds, increasing to speed 4. Still using the dough hook on speed 2, gradually add as much of the remaining milk as required to make a non-sticky dough. Cover the bowl and leave to stand in a warm, draft-free place for 45 minutes to 1 hour, until doubled in bulk.

2 Knead the dough for 1 to 2 minutes on speed 4, then separate into eight equal-size pieces and shape into dumplings the size of a snowball. Make a thumb imprint in the center of each dumpling and spoon a teaspoon of plum jam into each. Reshape the dumplings around the jam to encase completely. Put onto a cookie sheet lined with waxed paper and leave in a warm, draft-free place for a further 30 minutes.

3 Bring a large saucepan of water to a boil and add four of the dumplings. Cover and boil for 20 minutes until cooked through. Remove with a draining spoon and keep warm while cooking the remaining dumplings.

4 Meanwhile, heat the vanilla sugar and butter in a small saucepan until melted. Put the dumplings onto a warm plate and pour the butter and sugar mixture over just before serving.

TARTE AU CITRON
An exquisite lemon tart, which should be both sharp and sweet like the lemons it is made from. A sweet pastry is used here, though you could also use a plain rich shortcrust.

SERVES 6 TO 8

Preparation time: 15 minutes plus
2 hours chilling time
Cooking time: 35 minutes

Attachments used

1 quantity pâte sablée (page 119)

5 lemons, preferably unwaxed
5 medium eggs
1/4 tsp salt
1 1/4 cups superfine sugar
1 1/4 sticks butter (5 oz)
Confectioners' sugar, to dust

The best way to squeeze the juice out of your lemons is to use one hand to stabilize the KitchenAid mixer while juicing the fruit with your other hand. You can set the mixer bowl at a lower level to catch the juice, or place a glass or jug directly underneath the juicer.

1 Preheat the oven to 400°F. Roll the pastry out into a circle on a lightly floured surface and use to line a greased 10-inch loose-bottomed flan dish. Make a few holes in the pastry with a fork, fill with some dried beans, and blind bake for 10 minutes. Take out the beans and bake in the oven for a further 15 minutes. Remove the pastry case from the oven and take out of the dish. Set aside to cool.

2 Grate the rind from the lemons and reserve, then cut the lemons in half. Using the citrus juicer, on speed 6, squeeze out the juice and pour into a saucepan.

3 Bring the lemon juice to a boil. Meanwhile, place the eggs with the salt, sugar, and reserved lemon rind in the mixer bowl. Fit the wire whip and whisk well on speed 4. Still using the wire whip, gradually pour in the hot lemon juice while whisking. When all the lemon juice has been added, return to the cleaned saucepan and cook over a low heat, stirring continuously until the mixture thickens and coats the back of a wooden spoon.

4 Return the mixture to the cleaned mixer bowl and with the flat beater, on speed 6, gradually beat in the butter a little at a time. Pour the mixture into the pastry case and chill in the refrigerator for at least 2 hours before serving. Serve dusted with confectioners' sugar.

TARTE AU CHOCOLAT ET À LA FRAMBOISE Raspberries and chocolate

combine with a light lemon pastry in this classic French dessert – try replacing the raspberries with thin slices of mango or banana.

SERVES 6

Preparation time: 20 minutes plus 3 hours standing

Cooking time: About 30 minutes

Attachments used

For the lemon pastry

1²/₃ cups all-purpose flour

¹/₃ cup confectioners' sugar

Grated zest of ¹/₄ lemon

1¹/₄ sticks butter (5 oz)

3 Tbsp ground almonds

1 egg

Large pinch of salt

For the filling

9 oz dark chocolate

2 Tbsp sour cream

1 stick butter (¼ lb)

3 cups raspberries, cut in halves

1   Preheat the oven to 400°F. Place the flour, confectioners' sugar, lemon zest, butter, ground almonds, egg, and salt into the mixer bowl and, using the dough hook, mix on speed 1 to 2 until the pastry leaves the sides of the bowl clean. Shape into a ball, press down, and repeat two more times. Wrap in plastic wrap and leave to rest in a cool place for 3 hours.

2   To make the topping, melt the chocolate in a double boiler or in a heat proof bowl over, but not touching, a saucepan of boiling water. Place the sour cream in a small saucepan and bring almost to boiling, then pour into the melted chocolate. Cut the butter into small knobs and mix in.

3   Roll the pastry out into a circle on a lightly floured surface and use to line a greased tart pan. Make a few holes in the pastry with a fork, fill with some dried beans, and blind bake for 10 minutes. Take out the beans and bake in the oven for a further 15 minutes. Remove the pastry case from the oven and take out of the pan. Set aside to cool.

4   Arrange the raspberries in the bottom of the pastry case and cover with the chocolate mixture. Set aside for 30 minutes to cool, and then chill in the refrigerator for 1¹/₂ hours until the chocolate has set sufficiently to enable easy slicing.

POTS DE CRÈME AU CHOCOLAT
Delicious little chocolate custards, made with just cream and egg yolks, that are indulgently rich. Ramekins or martini glasses would also make stunning petits pots.

SERVES 6

Preparation time: 30 minutes plus 2 hours chilling time

Cooking time: 20 minutes

Attachments used

2 cups heavy cream (whipping cream)

1 Tbsp sugar

4 squares (1 oz each) chocolate, melted

3 egg yolks

1 Preheat the oven to 325°F. Heat the cream and the sugar in a double boiler or in a heatproof bowl over, but not touching, a saucepan of boiling water, stirring until the sugar has dissolved. Add the chocolate, stirring until well blended. Remove from the heat and set aside.

2 Place the egg yolks in the mixer bowl. Using the wire whip, on speed 8, whisk for 1 minute. Reduce to speed 2 and gradually add the cream mixture, whipping until well blended.

3 Fill six 2/3-cup custard cups or crème pots two-thirds full. Place the cups in a roasting pan and add enough boiling water to come halfway up the sides of the cups. Bake in the oven for 18 to 20 minutes or until firm. Chill for at least 2 hours before serving.

RAISIN CHEESECAKE

RAISIN CHEESECAKE This German version of the classic baked cheesecake is made with Quark, a fresh curd cheese that can be lower in fat than the cream cheese often used to make cheesecakes.

SERVES 10 TO 12

Preparation time: 15 minutes plus 30 minutes chilling time and cooling time

Cooking time: 1 hour 15 minutes

Attachments used

For the base

2 cups all-purpose flour

1 stick butter (¼ lb), softened

1/2 cup superfine sugar

1 egg

Pinch of salt

1 tsp baking powder

For the filling

3 cups Quark

1 cup sour cream

1 cup superfine sugar

4 eggs

Grated rind of half a lemon

1/4 tsp vanilla extract

3/4 cup raisins

1/4 cup cornstarch

1 tsp all-purpose flour

1 tsp baking powder

2 oz slivered almonds

1 To make the base, sift the flour into the mixer bowl. Add the butter, sugar, egg, salt, and baking powder, then, with the flat beater, mix on speed 2 for 2 minutes, until a smooth dough forms. Remove the dough from the bowl and wrap in a plastic bag. Chill for 30 minutes.

2 Preheat the oven to 375°F. Place all of the filling ingredients, except the almonds, in the mixer bowl and mix with the flat beater on speed 2 for 1 minute, until thoroughly combined.

3 Remove the dough from the refrigerator, roll out on a heavily floured surface, and use to line the base and sides of an 8-inch springform pan. Cook in the oven for 15 minutes.

4 Pour the filling into the partly cooked base and sprinkle the almonds over the top. Cook in the oven for 1 hour until cooked through. Turn the oven off and leave the cheesecake in the oven to cool. Serve chilled.

BLACK FOREST GATEAU (Schwarzwäldekirschtorte) This is a modern approach to the famous Black Forest

Gateau. Use fresh cherries if they are available, or canned, sour Morello cherries, making sure they are first thoroughly drained.

SERVES 8

Preparation time: 25 minutes plus overnight standing

Cooking time: 25 minutes

Attachments used

6 oz plain dark chocolate

6 Tbsp kirsch or brandy

1 cup superfine sugar

5 medium eggs, separated

1¼ cups heavy cream (whipping cream)

2–3 Tbsp confectioners' sugar

2 cups fresh cherries, pitted, or 14-oz can sour cherries (such as Morellos), drained

Extra cherries, to decorate

1 Preheat the oven to 350ºF. Lightly oil and line a jelly roll pan with waxed paper, ensuring that the paper stands about 2 inches above the sides of the pan.

2 Break the chocolate into small pieces and place in a double boiler or in a heatproof bowl over, but not touching, a saucepan of boiling water. Add 4 tablespoons of the kirsch or brandy and heat gently until the chocolate has melted. Stir until smooth, then remove from the heat.

3 Place the superfine sugar with the egg yolks in the mixer bowl and, using the wire whip on speed 8, beat until the mixture is very thick and creamy, then add the melted chocolate and beat again until thoroughly incorporated. Spoon into another bowl.

4 Clean the mixer bowl and the wire whip and dry thoroughly, then whisk the egg whites on speed 10, until very stiff. Fold 1 tablespoon of the egg white into the chocolate mixture and then carefully stir in the remaining egg white with a spoon. Stir lightly together, taking care not to over-mix, then turn into the prepared pan. Tap lightly on the surface to level it and to remove any air bubbles.

5 Bake in the oven for 20 to 25 minutes or until the top is set. Remove from the oven and cover with a damp sheet of waxed paper and a clean dish towel. Leave overnight or for at least 8 hours.

6 When ready to serve, whip the cream in the mixer bowl, using the wire whip on speed 8, and stir in the remaining kirsch or brandy. Sprinkle a large sheet of waxed paper with the confectioners' sugar and invert the cooked cake onto the iconfectioners' sugar paper. Remove the pan and discard the lining paper.

7 Spread with the whipped cream and top with the cherries, carefully roll up, and place on a serving plate. If you like, sprinkle with extra confectioners' sugar and decorate with the extra cherries.

DANISH CREAM PUDDING (Koldskaal) A Danish cream pudding made with buttermilk and vanilla that can be

poured over any soft fruit in season or just eaten with a spoonful of fruit jam. Serve with the kammerjunker cookies below.

MAKES 5 CUPS

Preparation time: 10 minutes

Attachments used

4 egg yolks

1/2 tsp vanilla extract

1/2 cup superfine sugar

Juice of half a small lemon

4 cups buttermilk

Quartered strawberries and sliced bananas, to serve

1 Put the egg yolks, vanilla extract, and sugar in the mixer bowl and, with the wire whip, whisk the ingredients together on speed 4, increasing to speed 6, for 2 to 3 minutes until frothy.

2 Still using the wire whip on speed 6, very slowly add the lemon juice until the mixture is very frothy. Increase to speed 8 and whisk for 1 minute. Return to speed 6 and gradually pour in the buttermilk until fully incorporated.

3 Divide the fruit among the serving dishes and spoon the koldskaal over the top. Serve with kammerjunker.

DANISH COOKIES (Kammerjunker) Hard, little Danish cookies, which are baked twice and can be served with a cream

dessert like the koldskaal above, ice cream, or a cup of coffee. This recipe makes 70 tiny cookies, which can be stored in an airtight container.

MAKES 70 SMALL COOKIES

Preparation time: 10 minutes

Cooking time: 35 minutes

Attachments used

3 cups all-purpose flour

1 stick butter, diced

1/2 cup superfine sugar

1 tsp baking powder

Grated rind of 1 lemon

1 egg

1/2 cup milk

1 Preheat the oven to 425°F. Sift the flour into the mixer bowl, add the butter, and, using the flat beater on speed 1, mix in until fully incorporated.

2 Add the sugar, baking powder, and lemon rind, and mix for a further 30 seconds. Lightly whisk the egg and milk together and blend into the mixture using the flat beater on speed 1. Continue to mix for 1 minute to knead the dough.

3 Turn out onto a floured surface and roll into thin 14-inch long sausages. Cut the dough into walnut-size balls and transfer to a nonstick cookie sheet. Cook in the preheated oven for 8 to 10 minutes until golden brown.

4 Remove the tray from the oven and cut the cookies in half. Return them to the oven, turn the oven off, and leave them to crisp in the remaining heat for 25 minutes. Serve with the koldskaal.

ALMOND PASTRIES

(Galettes à la Frangipane) Little round, flat cakes made here from flaky pastry and filled with a liqueur-soaked almond crème pâtissière. You could use ready-made pastry instead of making your own.

SERVES 4

Preparation time: 45 minutes plus 30 minutes chilling time

Cooking time: 20 minutes

Attachments used

4 Tbsp softened unsalted butter

³/₄ cup confectioners' sugar

2 egg yolks

³/₄ cup ground almonds

2 Tbsp liqueur, such as orange or pear liqueur, or rum

¹/₂ cup crème pâtissière (page 120)

1 lb flaky pastry (page 118)

For the glaze

1 egg

2 tsp confectioners' sugar

1 Put the butter into the mixer bowl. Sift over the confectioners' sugar and mix together with the flat beater on speed 1 until creamy. Beat in the egg yolks, one at a time.

2 Mix in the ground almonds and liqueur, then, with the machine still running, beat in the crème pâtissière a tablespoon at a time. Cover and chill until ready to use.

3 Roll out the pastry on a lightly floured surface to about 20 x 10 inches. Cut out eight 5-inch rounds, using a small bowl or saucer as a guide. Place four of the rounds on a large greased cookie sheet.

4 Spread a quarter of the almond filling in the center of each pastry round on the cookie sheet, leaving a border of about 1 inch all round. Brush the pastry borders with water, then place a second pastry round on top to enclose the filling. Press the edges together to seal, then flute or fork a pattern around the edge. Chill for at least 30 minutes.

5 Preheat the oven to 425°F. Make the glaze by beating the egg and confectioners' sugar together. Brush the tops of the pastries with the glaze, taking care not to allow it to run down the sides of the pastry or it will prevent them from rising evenly.

6 Using a small sharp knife, score the top of the pastry with long curved lines, starting at the center and ending at the edge, to make a spiral pattern. Make a small hole with a skewer in the center, to allow steam to escape during cooking.

7 Bake for 20 minutes, or until well-risen and golden brown. Allow to cool for 10 minutes before serving warm, or serve cold.

MERINGUES
To make perfect meringues, make sure the eggs are at room temperature and free of any trace of yolk and that the mixer bowl is scrupulously clean, as even a speck of fat can stop the eggs whisking properly.

To make incredibly crisp and light meringue, start whisking the egg whites slowly and turn the speed up gradually until soft peaks form that fall over when the wire whip is removed. After adding the sugar, whisk until the egg whites are shiny and stiff peaks form when the wire whip is removed.

MAKES 24 SMALL MERINGUES

Preparation time: 10 minutes

Cooking time: 3 hours

Attachments used

3/4 cup superfine sugar
3 Tbsp water
3 egg whites
Whipped cream, to serve

1 Preheat the oven to 250ºF. Put the sugar and water in a heavy-base saucepan and heat gently, stirring occasionally until the sugar has dissolved. Once the sugar has completely dissolved, bring the mixture to a boil and boil steadily until a light syrup is formed and a temperature is reached of 250ºF. Remove from the heat and reserve.

2 Put the egg whites into the mixer bowl and, using the wire whip, whisk on speed 4, increasing to 8, until the egg whites are stiff and soft peaks are formed.

3 Reduce the speed to 2, slowly pour in the prepared sugar syrup, and continue to whisk until the meringue is glossy and standing in stiff peaks. Spoon into a piping bag fitted with a large star nozzle and pipe 24 small meringues onto a cookie sheet lined with parchment baking paper. Cook for 2 1/2 to 3 hours until the meringues are dried out and cooked through.

4 Allow to cool, then sandwich the small meringues together with whipped cream.

STRAWBERRY AND PASSION FRUIT PAVLOVA This Australian

meringue dessert was named after the Russian ballerina Anna Pavlova and can be topped with any seasonal fresh fruit.

SERVES AT LEAST 8

Preparation time: 25 minutes

Cooking time: 2 hours

Attachments used

4 medium egg whites

Pinch of salt

1 cup superfine sugar

1 tsp vinegar

1 tsp cornstarch

1$\frac{1}{4}$ cups heavy cream (whipping cream)

4 cups strawberries (or a mixture of strawberries and raspberries)

2–3 passion fruit

1 Preheat the oven to 350°F. Using the wire whip, on speed 10, whisk the egg whites and salt until stiff. Whisking continuously, add the sugar a tablespoon at a time, beating well after each addition, until all the sugar has been added and the mixture is very stiff and shiny.

2 Sprinkle over the vinegar and the cornstarch and whisk on speed 4 for just a few seconds until they are incorporated into the mixture. Pile the mixture onto parchment baking paper on a cookie sheet and form into a circle approximately 8 inches in diameter.

3 Put the pavlova into the oven, then immediately reduce the heat to 300°F and leave it to cook for 2 hours. Turn off the oven and leave until it is completely cold.

4 Carefully peel the paper off the pavlova. You can now either leave the pavlova with the crunchy meringue on top, or turn it upside down and have the crunchy meringue at the bottom, so when you add your cream and fruit you have layers of textures – crunchy meringue, then marshmallow, then cream, and then the fruit.

5 Whip the cream in the mixer bowl with the wire whip at speed 4, then increase to speed 8. Place the cream on top and add the strawberries. Scoop the centers from the passion fruit and scatter the passion fruit seeds over the top so that some fall down the sides onto the serving plate.

APPLE STRUDEL
Once you have mastered this wafer-thin strudel pastry, try filling with cherries and cream cheese or a savory filling of ground meat or bacon mixed with vegetables.

SERVES 8 TO 10

Preparation time: 45 minutes plus 30 minutes standing time

Cooking time: 40 minutes

Attachments used

For the pastry

1 cup all-purpose flour

Pinch of salt

2 Tbsp butter or margarine

1 egg

3 Tbsp hot water

4 Tbsp butter, melted

For the filling

3¹/₄ lb tart apples (such as Granny Smith), peeled and cored

¹/₂ cup granulated brown sugar

¹/₂ cup chopped almonds

¹/₃ cup golden raisins

¹/₃ cup stale white bread crumbs

¹/₂ tsp ground cinnamon

1 Preheat the oven to 375°F. To make the pastry, sift the flour and salt into the mixer bowl. Cut the butter or margarine into cubes and add to the flour. Using the flat beater, on speed 1, beat until the butter is incorporated into the flour, then, still on speed 1, gradually add the egg and enough hot water to make a firm dough.

2 Change to the dough hook and knead on speed 4 for 2 minutes until smooth. Transfer the dough to a plastic bag and leave in a warm, draft-free place for 30 minutes.

3 To make the filling, slice the apples into the mixer bowl using the Rotor Slicer/Shredder, with the slicing drum attached, on speed 4. Stir in the sugar, almonds, raisins, bread crumbs, and cinnamon.

4 Put a clean dish towel on the work surface and sprinkle liberally with flour. Roll the dough out on the dish towel until you have rolled it as thinly as possible. Working quickly, begin to pull the dough over the back of your hands until it is wafer-thin. Do not let the dough go cold, otherwise it will crack.

5 Brush the dough with the melted butter, reserving some for glazing the strudel. Spread the filling evenly over the dough and, using the dish towel, roll it up into a long sausage shape. Transfer to a greased cookie sheet and brush the strudel with the remaining melted butter. Cook in the oven for 40 minutes until golden brown and cooked through, then serve warm with cream.

TARTE TATIN (Caramelized apple tart) A delicious French upside-down cake, served in bistros all over the country. Caramelized apples are baked with a pastry topping, then turned upside down to leave the buttery apples showing.

SERVES 8

Preparation time: 50 minutes plus 3 hours chilling time

Cooking time: 1 hour 20 minutes

Attachments used

1²/₃ cups all-purpose flour

Pinch of salt

2 sticks chilled butter (½ lb)

¹/₄ cup water

1 Tbsp lemon juice

For the filling

1 Tbsp water

³/₄ cup superfine sugar

6 Tbsp butter, cut into pieces

3¹/₄ lb tart apples (such as Granny Smith), peeled, cored, and sliced

1 Sift the flour and salt into the mixer bowl. Cut 2 tablespoons of the butter into cubes and add to the flour, then using the flat beater on speed 2, blend for 30 seconds.

2 Mix the water and lemon juice together. Using the flat beater on speed 2, pour the liquid into the bowl and mix to make a soft, elastic dough.

3 Shape the remaining butter into a rectangle between two sheets of plastic wrap or waxed paper and gently flatten to a 1-inch thickness.

4 Put the pastry dough onto a lightly floured surface and shape into a circle. Cut a cross in the center, cutting half the depth of the dough, and open out to form a star. Roll the dough out, keeping the center four times as thick as the edges. Put the flattened butter into the center and fold the dough over the top like an envelope, to encase completely.

5 Roll the dough into an 8 x 4-inch rectangle and fold the bottom third up to the center and the top third down. Seal the edges by pressing with the rolling pin, wrap the pastry in plastic wrap, and chill in the refrigerator for 30 minutes. Repeat the rolling, folding, and chilling process five more times, keeping the sealed edges to the left.

6 Preheat the oven to 350°F. To make the filling, put the water and ¹/₂ cup of the sugar in a small saucepan and heat over a low heat until it turns to a medium-brown caramel. Once it begins to color, keep a watchful eye as it will darken quickly. Pour the caramel into the base of a 10-inch nonstick shallow cake pan and cover with the butter and remaining sugar.

7 Arrange the apple pieces around the pan, starting from the outside and working into the center, and wedging them in closely. Place the pastry on top of the apples. Cook for 40 minutes in the oven, or until a knife is easily inserted into the fruit. Leave to cool completely.

APPLE PIE
The all-American apple pie, just like Mom makes. It has pastry underneath and on top. Use a tart apple, such as Granny Smith, as dessert apples become tough and chewy when cooked and tend to lose their flavor.

SERVES 8

Preparation time: 15 minutes plus 30 minutes chilling time

Cooking time: 30 minutes

Attachments used

For the pastry

2³/₄ cups all-purpose flour

Pinch of salt

2 Tbsp superfine sugar

1¹/₂ sticks unsalted butter (6 oz)

1 medium egg yolk

1 Tbsp cold water

Extra superfine sugar, for sprinkling

For the filling

1¹/₂ lb tart apples (such as Granny Smith)

1 Tbsp all-purpose flour

¹/₄ cup granulated brown sugar

1 Tbsp softened butter

1 Preheat the oven to 400°F. Sift the flour and salt into the mixer bowl and stir in the sugar. Cut the butter into cubes and add to the flour together with the egg yolk and cold water. Using the flat beater, on speed 2, beat for about 1 minute or until the mixture comes together and forms a ball in the center of the bowl. Remove, knead lightly on a lightly floured surface, then wrap, and chill in the refrigerator for 30 minutes.

2 To make the filling, peel and core the apples. Attach the slicing cone to the Rotor Slicer/Shredder and, on speed 4, slice the apples into a bowl. Add in the flour and brown sugar and stir lightly until the apples are well coated.

3 Knead the pastry on a lightly floured surface until smooth, then roll out half and use to line a deep 8-inch pie plate. Dampen the edges with cold water. Spoon in the apple and dot with the butter. Roll the remaining pastry out to form a lid and place on top of the apple. Trim the edges and press lightly together. Use any trimmings to decorate the top of the pie. Brush the top with a little water and sprinkle with superfine sugar.

4 Place on a cookie sheet and bake in the oven for 25 to 30 minutes, or until the pastry is golden brown. Remove from the oven, sprinkle with more sugar to taste, and serve with custard, cream, or ice cream.

LEMON AND LIME ICE CREAM
Italian gelato is made simply from cream, confectioners' sugar, and fresh juice. You could churn it in an ice-cream machine if you have one to give it a creamier texture. Lemon and lime here make a heavenly team.

SERVES 4 TO 6

Preparation time: 15 minutes plus freezing time

Attachments used

2 large lemons

2 limes

1¹/₄ cups confectioners' sugar

2¹/₂ cups heavy cream (whipping cream)

1 Using the coarse shredding cone on the Rotor Slicer/Shredder, shred the rind of all the fruit. Using the citrus juicer, on speed 6, juice the fruit and add to a bowl with the sugar and rind.

2 Pour the cream into the mixer bowl, attach the wire whip and pouring shield, and whisk the cream, slowly at first, then at speed 6 to 8. Halfway through whipping, add the juice, rind, and sugar and mix in until the cream is lightly whipped.

3 Turn into a shallow plastic container and freeze without a lid until firm, then cover. Before serving, place the container in the refrigerator for half an hour, to soften the ice cream and make it easier to scoop.

MANGO SORBET
A water ice made with ripe mangoes, this sorbet needs beating every hour to break up the large ice crystals, but it should still retain an icy, grainy texture. You can subsitute any really ripe soft fruit for the mango.

SERVES 4

Preparation time: 15 minutes plus freezing time

1 cup water

3/4 cup granulated sugar

2 large ripe mangoes, peeled, pitted, and cubed

Juice of a lemon

1 egg white, lightly beaten

Attachments used

1. Make a syrup by bringing the water and sugar to a boil, stirring to help dissolve the sugar. Simmer for a few minutes, then remove from the heat, and allow to cool.

2. Using the strainer, on speed 4, feed the pieces of mango through to obtain a thick purée. Then mix the purée with the syrup and lemon juice.

3. If you are using an ice-cream machine, follow the manufacturer's instructions, adding the egg white for the last 5 minutes of churning. If you do not have an ice cream machine, add the egg whites to the mango purée, then turn into a shallow plastic container.

4. Open-freeze the sorbet, removing every hour and beating to break up the ice crystals.

5. When almost frozen but still liquid in the center, tip the mixture into the mixer bowl and, using the flat beater, beat on speed 6 to 8 until free of ice crystals.

6. Before serving, place the container in the refrigerator for 1 hour to soften the ice cream and to make it easier to scoop out.

Before straining fruit or vegetables in the fruit/vegetable strainer, remove any thick skin or rind, such as that on apples and oranges, and any large seeds, hulls, or stems. If the fruit or vegetables are very tough you may prefer to cook them before straining, but make sure you adjust any cooking times in the recipes accordingly.

TIRAMISU An Italian dessert of sponge fingers soaked in espresso and topped with soft mascarpone cheese, whose name means literally

"pick me up." The addition of liqueur provides an extra dimension to the coffee flavor.

SERVES 8 TO 10

Preparation time: 15 minutes plus 4 to 6 hours
chilling time

8 eggs

3/4 cup confectioners' sugar

4 cups mascarpone (or for a lighter tiramisu: 2 cups mascarpone
    and 2 cups ricotta cheese)

30 sponge fingers

11/4 cups very strong or espresso coffee

1/3 cup cocoa powder

For a liqueur tiramisu

Add 1/2 Tbsp Marsala, brandy, rum, or Amaretto to the coffee

Attachments used

1 Put 4 eggs and 4 egg yolks, the sugar, and mascarpone in the mixer bowl and, with the wire whip on speed 2, mix for 30 seconds, increasing to speed 6 for 2 minutes until well combined.

2 Dip 15 sponge fingers into the coffee and use to line the base of a 10 x 6 x 2-inch dish. Cover with half the mascarpone mixture.

3 Dip the remaining sponge fingers into the coffee and layer over the mixture in the dish. Cover with the remaining mascarpone mixture.

4 Sprinkle the top with cocoa powder and refrigerate for 4 to 6 hours.

ZABAGLIONE This sweet creamy dessert is made from Marsala, a sweet Italian fortified wine, and egg yolks and sugar. It can be

enjoyed on its own or used as an alternative to cream and served with a dessert or flan.

SERVES 6

Preparation time: 10 minutes

6 egg yolks

3/4 cup confectioners' sugar, sifted

6 Tbsp Marsala

Attachments used

1 Put the egg yolks in the mixer bowl, then add the sugar and Marsala. Using the wire whip, mix on speed 8 for 5 minutes until creamy.

2 Increase the speed to 10 and whisk the mixture for 5 to 7 minutes until it is three times its original volume and only just pourable. Transfer immediately to six tall serving glasses or flutes, and serve.

RASPBERRY PARFAIT
A French iced dessert made from an egg custard, to which cream and fruit, chocolate, coffee, or a liqueur are added. A parfait is so smooth it can be cut into slices to serve. See note on Vanilla Sugar, Floating Islands (page 127).

SERVES 8

Preparation time: 10 minutes plus 2 hours 20 minutes freezing and standing time

Attachments used

4 eggs
2¹/₂ cups superfine sugar
¹/₂ tsp vanilla extract or 2 Tbsp vanilla sugar
Pinch of salt
¹/₂ cup heavy cream (whipping cream)
2 cups frozen raspberries

1 Put the eggs, sugar, vanilla extract or vanilla sugar, and salt into the mixer bowl and, using the wire whip, blend the ingredients together on speed 4 for 1 minute, until well combined. Spoon the mixture into another bowl.

2 Pour the cream into the mixer bowl and, using the wire whip, whisk on speed 8 for 1 minute until thick and peaking. Add the egg mixture and, using the wire whip, mix on speed 2 for 30 seconds.

3 Using the food grinder with the fine grinding plate attached, on speed 4, crush the raspberries into the mixture. Remove the food grinder, replace with the wire whip, and mix on speed 2 for 30 seconds until the raspberries are incorporated.

4 Transfer the parfait mixture to 8 individual molds or one 4-cup mold and freeze for at least 2 hours until solid. Remove the parfait from the freezer 20 minutes before serving to soften, then unmold onto a serving plate and slice.

FROZEN STRAWBERRY DAIQUIRI
This delicious iced drink is perfect to serve at a cocktail party as it is simple to make but looks and tastes stunning. For a mango daiquiri, substitute fresh mango and mango sorbet for the strawberries.

SERVES 1 TO 2

Preparation time: 5 minutes

Blender used

4 to 6 Tbsp white rum

$1/2$ tsp lime juice

1 tsp orange juice

3 fresh strawberries

2 scoops strawberry sorbet

Ice cubes

Slices of strawberry and mint leaves, to decorate

1 Combine the rum, lime juice, orange juice, strawberries, and the strawberry sorbet in the blender and process at liquefy speed to blend.

2 Pour the daiquiri over ice cubes in two glasses and serve decorated with slices of fresh strawberry and mint leaves.

MARGARITA
A Mexican lime cocktail that tastes wonderful with spicy tortillas and dips. Chill the cocktail glasses before use and coat the rims in a little salt. You can also use Cointreau instead of the triple sec liqueur.

SERVES 4

Preparation time: 10 minutes

Blender used

$3/4$ cup tequila

$1/2$ cup triple sec liqueur

$1/2$ cup fresh lime juice

$1^1/2$ Tbsp sugar

24 ice cubes

Lime wedge and salt, to serve

1 Place all the ingredients in the blender. Cover and blend at liquefy speed, pulsing six to eight times for about 15 seconds each time, until slushy.

2 Moisten the rim of the chilled cocktail glasses with a wedge of lime, then turn the glass into a saucer filled with salt to create a salt rim. Pour in the margarita and serve immediately.

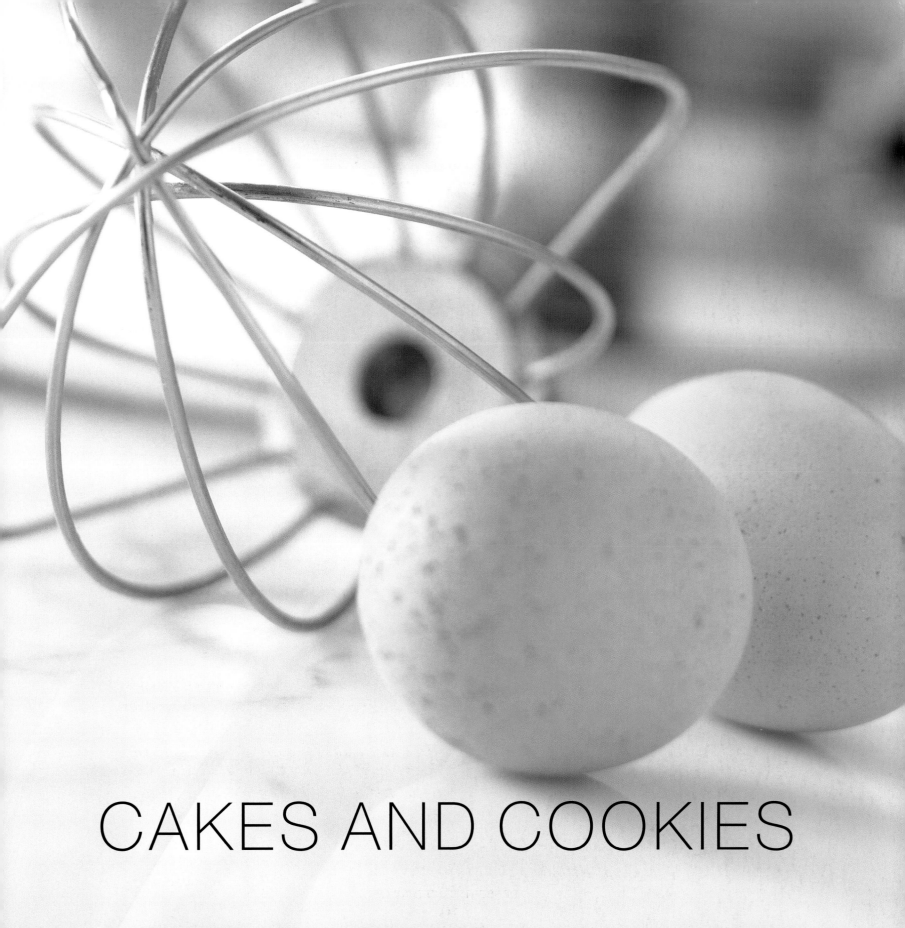

CAKES AND COOKIES

THE KITCHENAID BIRTHDAY CAKE
Your mixer is to hand for that special cake, and it couldn't be simpler. You can vary the flavor of this cake and the butter cream according to your preference, and then just decorate accordingly.

SERVES 8 TO 10

Preparation time: 30 minutes

Cooking time: 30 minutes

Attachments used

For the cake

1¹/₂ sticks softened unsalted butter (6 oz) or margarine

³/₄ cup superfine sugar

Grated rind of 1 lemon

3 medium eggs, beaten

1¹/₂ cups self-rising flour

¹/₄ cup ground almonds

For the butter cream

1 stick unsalted butter (¼ lb) or margarine

Grated rind of 1 lemon

1¹/₃ cups confectioners' sugar, sifted

1–2 Tbsp lemon juice

¹/₂ cup toasted slivered almonds

1¹/₄ cups confectioners' sugar

2–3 Tbsp lemon juice

Candles and candle holders

Sugar flowers, or other suitable decoration

1 Preheat the oven to 350ºF. Lightly oil and line two 8-inch, round baking pans with parchment baking paper. To make the cake, place the butter or margarine, the sugar, and lemon rind in the mixer bowl and, using the flat beater on speed 4, beat until light and fluffy. With the motor running, gradually add the eggs, beating well between each addition, and adding a spoonful of the flour after each addition.

2 When all the eggs have been added, add the remaining flour and the ground almonds, and beat briefly. Add 1 to 2 tablespoons of cooled boiled water if necessary to give a soft dropping consistency. Turn into the prepared pans and level the top.

3 Bake in the oven for 25 to 30 minutes, or until risen and golden brown, and the tops spring back when touched lightly with a fingertip. Remove from the oven and cool slightly, then turn out onto a wire rack. Leave until cold, then discard the lining paper.

4 Make the butter cream by beating the butter or margarine with the lemon rind in the mixer bowl, using the flat beater on speed 4. Gradually stir in the confectioners' sugar, beating well. Add the lemon juice to give a soft, spreadable consistency.

5 Spread about one-third of the butter cream over one of the cool sponges and place the other sponge on top. Press lightly together.

6 Reserving about 3 tablespoons of the butter cream, spread the remainder round the sides of the cake. Place the toasted almond slivers on a sheet of waxed paper, then roll the sides of the cake in the almonds. Put the cake on a serving plate or silver cake board.

7 Spoon the reserved butter cream into an icing bag fitted with a small star nozzle, and pipe a border round the edge of the cake.

8 To make the icing, sift the confectioners' sugar into the mixer bowl, then slowly add the lemon juice, stirring well until a smooth spreadable icing is formed. Pour over the top of the cake and allow to set. Decorate with the sugar flowers or other decorations and, if you like, pipe a greeting onto the set icing.

GUGELHOPF A slender ring-shaped cake popular all over Central Europe, from its origins in Alsace. This version is made with chocolate and marzipan and looks wonderful dusted with confectioners' sugar just before serving.

SERVES 14

Preparation time: 10 minutes

Cooking time: 35 minutes

Attachments used

2 sticks butter (½ lb) or margarine

$^1/_2$ cup superfine sugar

$2^1/_4$ cups all-purpose flour

1 tsp baking powder

5 eggs, beaten

4 oz dark chocolate, chopped small

5 oz marzipan, chopped small

4–6 drops almond oil

1 Preheat the oven to 400°F. Butter a 10-inch Gugelhopf pan or fluted ring mold and dust the inside with flour.

2 Put the butter or margarine and sugar in the mixer bowl and, with the flat beater, cream the ingredients on speed 4 for 30 seconds.

3 Mix the flour and baking powder together and, using the flat beater on speed 2, gradually add to the creamed mixture, alternating with the eggs, until all of the ingredients are combined. Stir the chocolate, marzipan, and the almond oil into the mixture.

4 Pour into the prepared pan and cook for 35 minutes until cooked through – a skewer inserted into the center of the cake should come out clean. Turn the cake out onto a wire rack and leave to cool before slicing.

GÂTEAU SAVOIE
A sponge cake from the mountainous region of Savoie in the French Alps, this gâteau has no added fat so it can be whisked with the wire whip, but should be eaten the day it is made.

SERVES 10

Preparation time: 10 minutes

Cooking time: 30 minutes

Attachments used

1¹/₄ cups superfine sugar

5 eggs

1 Tbsp water

Pinch of salt

³/₄ cup potato flour

³/₄ cup all-purpose flour

1   Preheat the oven to 375°F. Put the sugar in the mixer bowl and add one whole egg. Separate the remaining eggs and add the yolks to the bowl, reserving the egg whites. Add a tablespoon of water and the salt, and whisk well with the wire whip on speed 1 for one minute. Increase the speed to 6 and whisk for one further minute until the mixture is white. Transfer to another bowl.

2   Clean the mixer bowl and the wire whip and dry thoroughly, then whisk the egg whites on speed 8 until stiff, add the egg yolk mixture, and mix on speed 1 for 30 seconds until combined.

3   Sift the flours together and whisk into the mixture using the wire whip, on speed 1, for 30 seconds until combined.

4   Butter a deep 8-inch round cake pan and transfer the mixture to the pan. Cook in the oven for 30 to 40 minutes until golden brown and set – a skewer inserted in the center should come out clean. Turn the cake out onto a wire rack and leave to cool before slicing.

MARBLE CAKE

A very simple sponge cake made with two colors of cake mixture, here plain white and chocolate, combined together lightly at the end with a fork to create a marbled effect.

SERVES 12

Preparation time: 10 minutes

Cooking time: 1 hour

Attachments used

2 sticks butter (½ lb)

1¼ cups superfine sugar

4 eggs

4¼ cups all-purpose flour

2 tsp baking powder

3 cups milk

2 Tbsp cocoa powder

1 Preheat the oven to 350°F. Grease a deep 8-inch cake pan and set aside. Put the butter, sugar, and eggs in the mixer bowl and, with he flat beater, beat the mixture on speed 4 for 1 minute until creamy. Mix the flour and baking powder together and, still using the flat beater, gradually add to the mixture, alternately with the milk. Increase to speed 4 and mix for 2 minutes, until well combined.

2 Spoon two-thirds of the mixture into the prepared cake pan. Add the cocoa powder to the remainder in the mixer and, with the flat beater, blend on speed 2 for 30 seconds.

3 Pour the cocoa mixture into the cake pan and run a fork through to create a marbled effect. Bake in the oven for 1 hour or until cooked through – a skewer inserted in the center should come out clean. Leave to cool in the pan for 5 minutes before turning out onto a wire rack to cool completely.

ALMOND CAKES

(Torta di Mandorle) Almond cakes are made all over Europe, but this Sardinian version is particularly good, with a light whipped sponge covered with a rich almond icing spiked with Amaretto. See note on Vanilla Sugar, Floating Islands (page 127).

SERVES 6

Preparation time: 1 hour

Cooking time: 45 minutes

Attachments used

1 cup blanched almonds

1 lemon, preferably unwaxed

4 medium eggs, separated

$^1/_2$ cup superfine sugar

$^1/_4$ cup vanilla sugar

$^1/_2$ cup all-purpose flour

1 tsp baking powder

For the topping

$^1/_2$ cup blanched almonds

1 cup confectioners' sugar

2 Tbsp Amaretto (almond liqueur), optional

1 Preheat the oven to 350°F. Lightly oil an 11-inch round cake pan and dust with a little flour. Using the food grinder, fitted with the fine grinding plate, pass the blanched almonds into the mixer bowl on speed 4. Repeat this, to ensure that the almonds are chopped fine, then place in another bowl.

2 Finely shred the lemon rind from half the lemon and squeeze out and reserve the juice. Place the egg yolks into the mixer bowl with the superfine and vanilla sugars. Using the wire whip, whisk the mixture on speed 4 until doubled in size and very thick and foamy. Sift the flour and baking powder into the mixture, then stir in the almonds and lemon rind. Spoon into another bowl.

3 Clean the mixer bowl and the wire whip and dry thoroughly, then whisk the egg whites with $^1/_2$ teaspoon of the reserved lemon juice on speed 8 until stiff and softly peaking. Gradually stir into the egg yolk mixture, then spoon into the prepared cake pan and smooth the top.

4 Tap the pan lightly on the work surface to remove any air bubbles, then bake in the oven for 40 minutes or until the top feels firm to the touch. To test, insert a skewer into the center of the cake and leave for 30 seconds – if the skewer is clean when removed, the cake is cooked.

Remove from the oven and, when cool, remove from the pan and leave until cold before icing.

5 To make the icing, attach the Rotor Slicer/Shredder with the coarse shredding cone and, on speed 4, chop the almonds. Place in a skillet and toast lightly. Leave to cool.

6 Sift the confectioners' sugar into a bowl and gradually stir in 2 tablespoons of the reserved lemon juice and the liqueur if using (or more lemon juice) to form a smooth, spreadable icing. Spread over the cake and sprinkle with the chopped almonds. Leave to set before serving.

APRICOT STREUSEL CAKE
A streusel cake is a cake with a crumble topping made from butter, sugar, flour, and spices, here the topping being sprinkled over apricot halves before baking. See note on Vanilla Sugar, Floating Islands (page 127).

SERVES 12

Attachments used

Preparation time: 20 minutes

Cooking time: 35 minutes

2/3 cup low-fat curd cheese

4 Tbsp milk

4 Tbsp vegetable oil

1 egg

1/2 cup superfine sugar

1 Tbsp vanilla sugar

Pinch of salt

3 1/2 cups all-purpose flour

3 tsp baking powder

For the topping

1 2/3 cups all-purpose flour

2/3 cup superfine sugar

1 Tbsp vanilla sugar

1 1/4 sticks butter (5 oz)

1/2 tsp ground cinnamon

Three 14-oz cans apricot halves, drained

1 Preheat the oven to 350ºF. Put the cheese, milk, oil, egg, superfine sugar, vanilla sugar, and salt into the mixer bowl and, with the wire whip, combine the ingredients on speed 6 for 30 seconds until fully mixed.

2 Mix the flour and baking powder together and add half to the cheese mixture. Blend with the wire whip for 30 seconds on speed 2.

3 Change the wire whip for the dough hook and add the remaining flour. Knead for 3 minutes on speed 2 until the dough is smooth. Roll the dough out on a lightly greased cookie sheet to form a 12-inch circle.

4 To make the topping, put the flour, superfine sugar, vanilla sugar, and butter in the mixer bowl with the cinnamon and, with the flat beater, mix for 1 to 2 minutes on speed 4, until the mixture is crumbly. Arrange the apricot halves on top of the dough with the rounded side uppermost, then sprinkle the topping evenly over. Cook in the oven for 30 to 35 minutes until golden brown. Serve warm with cream or ice cream.

PLUM CAKE (Pflaumenkuchen) This simple plum cake is a specialty in Bavaria where it is made with tart Italian plums, which are less sweet and juicy than regular plums, and here lies its success. It can be made with any fruit and can also be made without its crumbled cinnamon top.

SERVES 8

Preparation time: 10 minutes

Cooking time: 40 minutes

Attachments used

1 stick butter (¼ lb)

1/3 cup superfine sugar

1/2 tsp vanilla extract

1 egg

Pinch of salt

1 Tbsp sour cream

1 tsp grated lemon rind

3 1/2 cups all-purpose flour

1 tsp baking powder

10 oz plums, pitted and halved

For the topping (optional)

2 Tbsp butter

2/3 cup all-purpose flour

1/3 cup superfine sugar

1/2 tsp ground cinnamon

Whipped cream, to serve

1 Preheat the oven to 375ºF. Put the butter, sugar, and vanilla extract into the mixer bowl and, with the flat beater, mix on speed 4 to blend the mixture for 30 seconds. Add the egg, salt, sour cream, and lemon rind, and mix on speed 4 for a further 30 seconds. Mix the flour and baking powder together and add to the bowl, mixing on speed 2 for 1 minute until the dough comes together.

2 Lightly grease a shallow 8-inch round cake pan and press the dough into the base. Arrange the plum halves, cut side up, on top of the dough.

3 To make the topping, put the butter, flour, sugar, and cinnamon into the mixer bowl and, using the flat beater, blend the mixture on speed 4 for 30 seconds until crumbly. Sprinkle the mixture over the plums evenly and cook in the oven for 30 to 40 minutes until golden brown. Serve warm or cold, topped with fresh whipped cream.

SACHERTORTE

A rich Viennese chocolate cake that needs to be made a day in advance and has a coating of apricot jam and a smooth, dark icing. It traditionally also has the word "Sacher" piped in chocolate across the top.

SERVES 12

Preparation time: 40 minutes plus overnight standing

Cooking time: 1 hour 10 minutes

Attachments used

5 oz dark chocolate

1¼ sticks butter (5 oz)

¾ cup confectioners' sugar, sifted

6 eggs, separated

⅓ cup superfine sugar

1¼ cups all-purpose flour

3 Tbsp apricot jam

For the icing

4 oz dark chocolate

4 Tbsp butter

⅓ cup confectioners' sugar, sifted

2 Tbsp hot water

1 Preheat the oven to 350°F. Heat the chocolate and butter for the cake in a double boiler or in a heatproof bowl over, but not touching, a saucepan of boiling water. Stir and allow to cool a little. Gradually stir in the confectioners' sugar and egg yolks.

2 Put the egg whites in the mixer bowl and, using the wire whip, whisk on speed 8 for 1 minute until they are stiff and peaking. Still using the wire whip on speed 8, add the superfine sugar, a tablespoon at a time, until the mixture is peaking again.

3 Transfer the chocolate mixture to a large bowl and carefully stir in a spoonful of the egg whites. Add the remaining egg white to the mixture with alternate spoons of flour, folding in gently.

4 Grease a 9-inch deep cake pan and dust with a little flour. Pour the cake mixture into the pan and cook for 10 minutes with the oven door slightly open. Reduce the oven temperature to 300°F, and cook for 50 minutes until the cake is cooked through. Remove the cake from the oven, cover with a clean dish towel, and leave to cool until the following day.

5 Remove the cake from the pan. Sift the apricot jam into a small saucepan and warm through. Brush the jam over the top and sides of the cake.

6 Melt the chocolate and butter for the icing in a double boiler or in a heatproof bowl over, but not touching, a saucepan of boiling water, and stir in the confectioners' sugar and water. Beat well and leave to stand for 5 minutes before spreading over the top and sides of the cake. Leave to cool before serving.

ORANGE CHIFFON CAKE
This very light American cake is made with oil instead of butter. To cut it, you'll need a long serrated knife and to use a gentle sawing motion.

SERVES 6 TO 8

Preparation time: 30 minutes

Cooking time: 1 hour 15 minutes

Attachments used

$2^{1}/_{4}$ cups self-rising flour

3 tsp baking powder

1 tsp salt

$1^{1}/_{2}$ cups superfine sugar

$^{1}/_{2}$ cup vegetable oil

5 egg yolks, at room temperature

3 Tbsp grated orange zest

$^{3}/_{4}$ cup orange juice

8 egg whites, at room temperature

$^{1}/_{2}$ tsp cream of tartar

For the orange glaze

$^{1}/_{2}$ cup orange juice

4–5 Tbsp sugar

1 Preheat the oven to 325°F. Sift the flour, baking powder, and salt into the mixer bowl and add the sugar. Make a well in the center and add the oil, egg yolks, and orange zest. Using the flat beater on speed 2, beat for 30 seconds, then stop and scrape the bowl. Add the orange juice, turn to speed 6, and beat for 1 minute. Remove the mixture from the bowl and set aside.

2 Clean the mixer bowl and dry thoroughly, then add the egg whites and the cream of tartar, and attach the wire whip. Whisk, on speed 8, until stiff but not dry. Fold the flour mixture into the egg whites, one-third at a time, until blended.

3 Pour the batter into an ungreased 10-inch ring mold. Bake in the oven for 55 minutes. Increase the oven temperature to 350°F and bake for 10 minutes longer. Turn the cake upside down on a wire rack to cool.

4 To make the orange glaze, place the orange juice and sugar in a small saucepan. Bring to a boil over a medium heat and stir until thickened slightly. Remove from the heat and allow to cool.

5 Remove the cake from the mold by gently loosening all the edges with a knife. Place on a serving plate and drizzle the orange glaze over the top.

WALNUT CAKE WITH SYRUP
This Greek cake, made with walnuts and coated with a cinnamon-sugar syrup, is baked to be enjoyed with a small cup of strong Greek coffee.

SERVES 8

Preparation time: 1 hour

Cooking time: 1 hour 10 minutes

Attachments used

4 cups walnuts

4 slices day-old white bread, crusts discarded

1$^1/_4$ sticks unsalted butter (5 oz)

4 medium eggs, separated

$^2/_3$ cup superfine sugar

1$^1/_2$ Tbsp baking powder

1 Tbsp ground cinnamon

$^2/_3$ cup cognac

For the syrup

2 cups sugar

2$^1/_2$ cups water

Cinnamon stick, lightly bruised

Large pieces of thinly pared lemon rind

1 Preheat the oven to 350°F. Lightly oil and line an 8-inch deep cake pan with parchment baking paper. With the coarse grinding plate on the grinder, on speed 4, grind the nuts and then the bread into crumbs. Reserve both separately.

2 Place the butter in the mixer bowl. Using the flat beater, on speed 6, beat until soft and creamy. Add the egg yolks one at a time, beating well after each addition. When all the egg yolks have been added, stir in the sugar and continue to beat until the mixture is well combined.

3 Sift the baking powder into the mixture, then add the bread crumbs and the ground cinnamon. Beat for 1 minute until well mixed. Turn into another bowl.

4 Clean the mixer bowl and dry thoroughly then, using the wire whip, on speed 10, whisk the egg whites until stiff and standing in peaks. Carefully stir into the blended mixture alternately with the chopped walnuts and the cognac.

5 Stir gently until thoroughly mixed, then spoon into the prepared cake pan and level the top. Bake in the oven for 1 hour. Remove and allow to cool before taking out of the pan.

6 To make the syrup, place the sugar and the water in a heavy-base saucepan and heat gently until the sugar has dissolved. Add the cinnamon stick and lemon rind, and bring to a boil. Boil steadily for 5 minutes or until a light syrup is formed. Remove the cinnamon stick and lemon rind. Pour the warm syrup over the cake and leave until cold before serving.

APPLE FRITTERS
(Buñuelos de Manzana) Irresistible apple fritters are made with whole pieces of apple, marinated in an aniseed liqueur and deep-fried in batter until crisp and golden. They need to be eaten as soon as they are cooked, dusted with sugar.

MAKES 32

Preparation time: 40 minutes plus 1 hour standing time

Cooking time: 5 minutes

Attachments used

3 Tbsp anisette or Pernod

1/2 cup superfine sugar

8 dessert apples, peeled, cored, and cut into rings

4 eggs

11/4 cups milk

23/4 cups all-purpose flour

1 heaping tsp active dry yeast

2 tsp salt

2 Tbsp all-purpose flour, for coating

Oil, for deep-frying

Confectioners' sugar, for dusting

1 Mix the anisette and sugar together in a bowl and toss the apple rings into the mixture. Set aside for 30 minutes.

2 Put the eggs and milk in the mixer bowl and, with the flat beater, mix on speed 2 for 30 seconds. Add the flour, yeast, and salt, and mix for 1 minute on speed 4. Leave the batter to rest for an hour.

3 Drain the apples and toss them in the coating flour, then roll in the batter to coat them well.

4 Heat a deep pan of oil to 350°F and cook the apples in four batches for 1 minute until golden brown. Remove from the oil with a slotted spoon, drain on paper towels, and keep warm while cooking the remaining apples. Dust the fritters with confectioners' sugar and serve warm.

COCONUT MACAROONS
These little macaroons, a favorite of French pâtisseries, are made from coconut rather than the more usual ground almonds. They can be served with a dessert wine or an ice cream or mousse.

MAKES ABOUT 30 MACAROONS
Preparation time: 10 minutes
Cooking time: 35 minutes

Attachments used

4 egg whites
1/4 tsp cream of tartar
1 1/4 cups superfine sugar
1 tsp lemon juice or white wine vinegar
1 tsp vanilla extract
3 cups desiccated coconut

1 Preheat the oven to 300°F. Line two cookie sheets with parchment baking paper.

2 Using the wire whip on speed 4, beat the egg whites until frothy. Add the cream of tartar and beat on speed 10 until stiff peaks form. Whisking continuously, add the sugar 2 tablespoons at a time, beating well after each addition, until all the sugar has been added and the mixture is very stiff and shiny.

3 Sprinkle the lemon juice or vinegar, vanilla extract, and coconut over the meringue mixture. Whisk on speed 4 for just a few seconds until incorporated into the mixture.

4 Drop heaped teaspoons of the mixture onto the prepared cookie sheets, spacing them slightly apart. Bake for 30 to 35 minutes, until the macaroons are light golden and the insides are still slightly soft.

5 Leave on the cookie sheets for 5 minutes, then transfer to a wire rack to cool. Store in an airtight container.

SHORTBREAD
This rich Scottish cookie is traditionally cut into wedges called "petticoat tails." For an even shorter texture, you can substitute 3/4 cup of the flour for an equal amount of ground rice or rice flour.

MAKES 16 WEDGES
Preparation time: 10 minutes
Cooking time: 30 minutes

Attachments used

1/2 cup confectioners' sugar
1/4 cup superfine sugar
1 1/2 sticks butter (6 oz), softened
2 3/4 cups all-purpose flour

1 Preheat the oven to 300°F. Sift the confectioners' sugar into the mixer bowl. Add the superfine sugar and butter, and use the flat beater, on speed 1, to mix them together. Increase to speed 6 and beat the mixture until it is pale and fluffy.

2 Sift the flour over the mixture and mix on speed 2 until it resembles large bread crumbs.

3 Gather the dough together with your hands and divide equally between two 8-inch loose-bottom cake pans, lightly pressing it until even with the back of a spoon. Using a fork, mark a pattern around the edges, then lightly prick the surface all over.

4 Bake for 30 minutes, or until the shortbread is a pale golden color, rotating the pans halfway through cooking. Mark the surface of each into eight wedges while the shortbread is still warm and soft.

5 Leave to cool in the pans on a wire rack, then remove the rims from the pans, cut the shortbread into wedges, and store in an airtight container.

LEBKUCHEN
There are lots of varieties of these little German cakes made with honey and spices and glazed after baking.

A little like gingerbread, they are often served as a Christmas treat.

MAKES 24

Preparation time: 35 minutes plus at least 8 hours chilling time

Cooking time: 30 minutes

Attachments used

1 cup clear honey

$^3/_4$ cup dark brown sugar

1 egg, beaten

1 Tbsp lemon juice

1 tsp grated lemon rind

$2^3/_4$ cups all-purpose flour

1 tsp ground cinnamon

$^1/_2$ tsp ground allspice

$^1/_2$ tsp ground cloves

$^1/_2$ tsp ground nutmeg

$^1/_2$ tsp salt

$^1/_2$ tsp baking powder

$^1/_3$ cup candied chopped lemon

$^1/_2$ cup chopped almonds

Rice paper or parchment baking paper

12 candied cherries, halved, for decoration

1 cup blanched almonds, for decoration

$^2/_3$ cup confectioners' sugar, to glaze

2–3 Tbsp rum, to glaze

1 Heat the honey in a saucepan until it begins to bubble. Remove from the heat and stir in the brown sugar, egg, lemon juice and rind, and set aside.

2 Put the flour, spices, salt, and baking powder into the mixer bowl. With the flat beater, on speed 2, add the honey mixture and mix until well blended. Stir in the candied lemon and chopped almonds and leave to stand in the refrigerator for at least 8 hours and up to 24 hours if possible.

3 Preheat the oven to 375°F. Working with a quarter of the dough at a time, and keeping the remainder refrigerated, roll the dough out on a heavily floured work surface to a $^1/_2$-inch thickness. Cut 4-inch rounds

of rice paper or parchment baking paper and space 2 inches apart on a cookie sheet.

4 Cut out 3-inch rounds from the dough and place one onto each paper base. Put a cherry half into the center of each and arrange five almonds around the cherry to represent flower petals. Cook in two batches in the oven for 12 to 15 minutes each batch. Repeat with the remaining dough.

5 Make up the glaze by mixing the confectioners' sugar and rum, and spread over the cakes after cooking. Leave to cool.

AUSTRIAN PASTRIES (Topfenkolatsche) These Austrian pastries are made with cream cheese rather than curd cheese, though you could use either. A wonderful sweet breakfast or afternoon treat.

MAKES 10

Preparation time: 1 hour, plus
2 hours 15 minutes standing time

Cooking time: 30 minutes

Attachments used

For the pastry

3¹/₂ cups all-purpose flour

Pinch of salt

1 heaping tsp active dry yeast

¹/₂ cup warm milk

2 Tbsp superfine sugar

1 egg

2 Tbsp butter, melted

For the filling

2 Tbsp butter

1 cup cream cheese

2 eggs, separated

¹/₂ cup superfine sugar

Grated rind of 1 lemon

1 Tbsp raisins

1 egg white, lightly beaten, for brushing

2 Tbsp chopped almonds

1 Sift the flour and salt for the pastry into the mixer bowl and add the yeast, warm milk, sugar, and egg. With the dough hook, mix on speed 4 for 1 minute until well blended. Changing to speed 2, add the melted butter in a stream. Cover the bowl and leave to stand for 1 hour 30 minutes, until doubled in size.

2 Put the dough on a lightly floured work surface and roll out to a ¹/₂-inch thickness. Cut into 3-inch squares and transfer to a cookie sheet.

3 To make the filling, put the butter, cream cheese, egg yolks, sugar, lemon rind, and raisins in the mixer bowl, fit the flat beater and mix on speed 4 for 30 seconds until soft. Transfer to a small bowl.

4 Clean the mixer bowl and dry thoroughly, then attach the wire whip and on speed 8 whisk the egg whites until stiff. Add the cream cheese mixture and blend with the flat beater on speed 2 until combined.

5 Put a tablespoon of filling into the center of each pastry square and fold the corners in to cover the filling, sealing the edges by pinching together. Leave to rise in a warm, draft-free place for 45 minutes.

6 Heat the oven to 350°F. Brush the pastries with egg white and sprinkle the almonds on top. Cook for 30 minutes until brown.

BLUEBERRY MUFFINS

These all-American muffins are so quick to prepare that you can bake them when you wake up for a weekend breakfast. Eat them when fresh and try making a batch using raspberries instead of blueberries.

MAKES 16

Preparation time: 10 minutes

Cooking time: 30 minutes

Attachments used

2^1/$_2$ cups blueberries

2 cups all-purpose flour

2^1/$_2$ tsp baking powder

^{1}/$_2$ tsp salt

^{1}/$_4$ tsp ground nutmeg

1 cup superfine sugar

2 eggs

^{3}/$_4$ cup milk

1 stick butter (^{1}/$_4$ lb), melted

Grated rind of 1 orange

1 tsp vanilla extract

^{1}/$_4$ cup granulated sugar

^{1}/$_4$ tsp ground nutmeg

1 Preheat the oven to 375°F. Line two muffin tins with 16 paper cups or lightly grease with butter.

2 Mash about 50 of the blueberries with a potato masher or fork. Sift the flour, baking powder, salt, and nutmeg into the mixer bowl. Stir in the sugar and make a well in the center.

3 With the flat beater, on speed 2, beat the eggs, milk, melted butter, orange rind, vanilla extract, and mashed blueberries into the flour, mixing for 30 seconds and being careful not to overmix. Gently mix in the remaining blueberries and spoon the mixture into the prepared pans, almost filling to the top with mixture.

4 Mix the granulated sugar and ground nutmeg together and sprinkle over the muffins. Cook in the oven for 25 to 30 minutes until risen and golden. Remove from the oven and cool in the pan for 5 minutes before transferring to a wire rack to cool.

GOLDEN RAISIN SCONES
Scones served with jam and spoonfuls of whipped cream are an essential part of British afternoon tea and are easy and quick to make. For a change, you could replace the raisins with dried apricots or dried cranberries.

MAKES 8

Preparation time: 10 minutes

Cooking time: 10 minutes

Attachments used

2 cups self-rising flour

Pinch of salt

$^1/_2$ stick unsalted butter (2 oz) or margarine

2 Tbsp superfine sugar

$^1/_3$ cup golden raisins

About $^2/_3$ cup milk

Milk, to glaze

Butter or cream and jam, to serve

1 Preheat the oven to 450°F. Lightly oil a cookie sheet. Sift the flour and salt into the mixer bowl and add the butter or margarine, the sugar, and golden raisins.

2 Using the flat beater, on speed 2, beat until the butter or margarine has been blended in. Still on speed 2, gradually pour in the milk until the mixture forms a ball in the center of the bowl.

3 Turn out onto a very lightly floured surface and knead briefly to remove any cracks. Gently roll out to 1 inch thick and cut out 1-inch rounds with a pastry cutter dipped into flour.

4 Place on the oiled cookie sheet and brush the tops with a little milk. Bake in the oven for 8 to 10 minutes, or until well risen and golden brown. Serve with butter or cream and jam.

DOUBLE CHOCOLATE BROWNIES
These sumptuous brownies can be cut into small squares for a snack or served in larger pieces with ice cream and a drizzle of melted chocolate for dessert.

MAKES ABOUT 20 SQUARES

Preparation time: 20 minutes

Cooking time: 30 minutes

Attachments used

10 oz good dark chocolate

1³/₄ sticks butter (7 oz)

1 cup superfine sugar

3 eggs

2 Tbsp Frangelico liqueur (optional)

6 Tbsp self-rising flour

¹/₂ cup roasted hazelnuts, chopped

²/₃ cup white chocolate chips

1 Preheat the oven to 375°F. Grease and line the base of a 9-inch square baking pan with parchment baking paper.

2 Break the chocolate into small pieces and place in a double boiler or in a heatproof bowl over, but not touching, a saucepan of boiling water. Add the butter and heat until melted.

3 Beat the sugar and eggs thoroughly using the flat beater on speed 4, then, with the motor still running, gradually drizzle in the melted chocolate mixture and the Frangelico if you are using it. Allow to cool slightly, then add the flour and hazelnuts, and mix with the flat beater on speed 4 to combine. Finally, add the white chocolate chips and fold in briefly on speed 2.

4 Pour the mixture into the prepared pan and bake for about 25 to 30 minutes or until just set. Remove from the oven and allow to cool in the pan.

SPEKULATIUS
These spicy Austrian cookies, flavored with cinnamon and almonds and cut into star shapes for Christmas, make enchanting gifts or decorations. Dust again with confectioners' sugar before serving.

MAKES 30

Preparation time: 15 minutes

Cooking time: 30 minutes

Attachments used

3 egg whites

1³/₄ cups confectioners' sugar, sifted

2 tsp vanilla extract

1 tsp ground cinnamon

2 drops almond extract

4 cups ground almonds

1–2 tsp cold water

Confectioners' sugar, for icing and dusting

1 Preheat the oven to 275ºF. Line a cookie sheet with parchment baking paper. Put the egg whites into the mixer bowl and using the wire whip, whisk the egg whites on speed 8 until stiff and peaking. Remove 1 heaping tablespoon of egg white for glazing, and reserve. Reduce to speed 2 and stir in the confectioners' sugar, 1 to 2 tablespoons at a time.

2 Add the vanilla extract, ground cinnamon, almond extract, and half of the ground almonds to the mixture, using the wire whip on speed 2. Add enough of the remaining almonds to give a fairly stiff dough.

3 Dust a work surface with confectioners' sugar and roll the dough out to ¹/₄-inch thickness. Using a star-shaped cookie cutter, cut stars from the dough, kneading and rerolling until it has all been used up.

4 Transfer the stars to the cookie sheet. Mix the reserved egg white with the cold water and brush over the top of the cookies. Bake in the oven for 25 to 30 minutes, then cool on a wire rack.

5 Once cooled, spread with white icing or dust the cookies with confectioners' sugar just before serving. Store in an airtight container until ready to eat.

BISCOTTI

Small Italian almond cookies that are hard and crunchy, and made to be dipped into a glass of vin santo, Tuscan dessert wine, at the end of a special meal.

MAKES ABOUT 60

Preparation time: 15 minutes

Cooking time: 35 minutes

Attachments used

2 cups slivered almonds

2 tsp butter, for greasing

3 medium eggs, separated

1¼ cups superfine sugar

Pinch of salt

Grated rind of 1 lemon

3½ cups all-purpose flour

3 tsp baking powder

1 Preheat the oven to 350°F. Place the almonds on a non-stick baking sheet and toast in the preheated oven for 5 to 10 minutes or until golden. Remove and cool. Lightly grease two cookie sheets with butter.

2 Put the egg yolks and sugar into the mixer bowl and fit the flat beater. Beat the mixture on speed 4 for 30 seconds. Transfer to another bowl.

3 Clean the mixer bowl and dry thoroughly, then attach the wire whip and whisk the egg whites and salt on speed 8 until peaking. Still using the wire whip, on speed 4, gradually add the egg yolk mixture until fully incorporated. Grate the rind of the lemon into the mixture, and add the toasted almonds. Fit the dough hook, and mix the dough on speed 4 for 30 seconds. Add the flour, baking powder, and butter. Continue to mix on speed 4 for a further minute to knead the dough.

4 Place the dough on a lightly floured surface and roll into four 1-inch wide sausage shapes. Transfer to the cookie sheets and bake in the preheated oven for 15 minutes until the edges have begun to turn golden brown.

5 Remove from the oven and immediately cut into ½-inch thick slices, cutting on the diagonal. Cool on wire cooling racks. Store once cold in an airtight container.